INSIDE THE MINDS

Driving Company Growth

Top CEOs on Developing a Vision, Adding Value, and Creating a Financial Impact

BOOK IDEA SUBMISSIONS

If you are a C-Level executive or senior lawyer interested in submitting a book idea or manuscript to the Aspatore editorial board, please email authors@aspatore.com. Aspatore is especially looking for highly specific book ideas that would have a direct financial impact on behalf of a reader. Completed books can range from 20 to 2,000 pages – the topic and "need to read" aspect of the material are most important, not the length. Include your book idea, biography, and any additional pertinent information.

SPEAKER SUBMISSIONS FOR CONFERENCES

If you are interested in giving a speech for an upcoming ReedLogic conference (a partner of Aspatore Books), please email the ReedLogic Speaker Board at speakers@reedlogic.com. If selected, speeches are given over the phone and recorded (no travel necessary). Due to the busy schedules and travel implications for executives, ReedLogic produces each conference on CD-ROM, then distributes the conference to bookstores and executives who register for the conference. The finished CD-ROM includes the speaker's picture with the audio of the speech playing in the background, similar to a radio address played on television.

INTERACTIVE SOFTWARE SUBMISSIONS

If you have an idea for an interactive business or software legal program, please email software@reedlogic.com. ReedLogic is specifically seeking Excel spreadsheet models and PowerPoint presentations that help business professionals and lawyers accomplish specific tasks. If idea or program is accepted, product is distributed to bookstores nationwide.

Published by Aspatore, Inc.

For corrections, company/title updates, comments, or any other inquiries, please e-mail store@aspatore.com.

First Printing, 2005
10 9 8 7 6 5 4 3 2 1

ISBN 1-59622-297-2
Library of Congress Control Number: 2005933126

Inside the Minds Managing Editor, Laura Kearns, Edited by Eddie Fournier, Proofread by Brian Denitzio

Praise for *Inside the Minds*

"What C-level executives read to keep their edge and make pivotal business decisions. Timeless classics for indispensable knowledge." - Richard Costello, Manager of Corporate Marketing Communication, General Electric

"Want to know what the real leaders are thinking about now? It's in here." - Carl Ledbetter, SVP & CTO, Novell, Inc.

"Priceless wisdom from experts at applying technology in support of business objectives." - Frank Campagnoni, CTO, GE Global Exchange Services

"Unique insights into the way the experts think and the lessons they've learned from experience." - MT Rainey, Co-CEO, Young & Rubicam/Rainey Kelly Campbell Roalfe

"A must-read for anyone in the industry." - Dr. Chuck Lucier, Chief Growth Officer, Booz-Allen & Hamilton

"Unlike any other business books, *Inside the Minds* captures the essence, the deep-down thinking processes, of people who make things happen." - Martin Cooper, CEO, Arraycomm

"A must-read for those who manage at the intersection of business and technology." - Frank Roney, General Manager, IBM

"A great way to see across the changing marketing landscape at a time of significant innovation." - David Kenny, Chairman & CEO, Digitas

"An incredible resource of information to help you develop outside the box..." - Rich Jernstedt, CEO, Golin/Harris International

"A snapshot of everything you need to know..." - Larry Weber, Founder, Weber Shandwick

"Great information for both novices and experts." - Patrick Ennis, Partner, ARCH Venture Partners

"The only useful way to get so many good minds speaking on a complex topic." - Scott Bradner, Senior Technical Consultant, Harvard University

"Must-have information for business executives." - Alex Wilmerding, Principal, Boston Capital Ventures

www.Aspatore.com

Aspatore Books is the largest and most exclusive publisher of C-level executives (CEO, CFO, CTO, CMO, partner) from the world's most respected companies and law firms. Aspatore annually publishes a select group of C-level executives from the Global 1,000, top 250 law firms (partners and chairs), and other leading companies of all sizes. C-Level Business Intelligence™, as conceptualized and developed by Aspatore Books, provides professionals of all levels with proven business intelligence from industry insiders–direct and unfiltered insight from those who know it best–as opposed to third-party accounts offered by unknown authors and analysts. Aspatore Books is committed to publishing an innovative line of business and legal books, those which lay forth principles and offer insights that when employed, can have a direct financial impact on the reader's business objectives, whatever they may be. In essence, Aspatore publishes critical tools–need-to-read as opposed to nice-to-read books–for all business professionals.

Inside the Minds

The critically acclaimed *Inside the Minds* series provides readers of all levels with proven business intelligence from C-level executives (CEO, CFO, CTO, CMO, partner) from the world's most respected companies. Each chapter is comparable to a white paper or essay, and is a future-oriented look at where an industry/profession/topic is heading and the most important issues for future success. Each author has been carefully chosen through an exhaustive selection process by the *Inside the Minds* editorial board to write a chapter for this book. *Inside the Minds* was conceived in order to give readers actual insights into the leading minds of business executives worldwide. Because so few books or other publications are actually written by executives in industry, *Inside the Minds* presents an unprecedented look at various industries and professions never before available.

Driving Company Growth

Top CEOs on Developing a Vision, Adding Value, and Creating a Financial Impact

CONTENTS

Establishing a Vision for the Organization

Richard C. Breon
President and Chief Executive Officer
Spectrum Health

Setting the Roadmap

As chief executive officer (CEO) of a large health care organization, my main task is to develop and set the vision of the organization—the roadmap of where we want to go. By doing this, I help develop the culture that gets us on that road. I see myself as a leader who must be visible and help our employees see the big picture. Maintaining focus of that broad vision gets people excited about the future, especially with 13,000 employees in one geographic area.

Part of keeping people excited about our vision is making sure we're visible in the community. I recently made a speech before our local Economic Club, a group of about 600 business leaders. I talked about making our organization a destination place for health care. The challenge is always in making what we do simple for other businesses to understand. I laid that out in a relatively short speech, but it resonated with the audience. Getting that message out to the business community, the media, and employees helps to carry it on and give it weight.

We have forty to fifty new employees starting here every week, so our orientation process is very important. We have incorporated our key messages and vision into orientation, so new employees learn who we are and what we're trying to be from the outset. People have to understand their specific responsibilities, but it's also important to see the broad scope. We have a wide variety of people, from physicians and people with Ph.D.s to high school graduates. This range of employees can only be unified by a consistent message that imparts vision and excitement throughout the company.

The task of the CEO is to set that vision, hire the right people, and get out of the way. I see my role as setting the tone, getting the right people in place, and allowing them to do what they do best. We have some incredibly talented managers and very well educated people from all across the country. They must be in a flexible environment where they are able to make decisions. If you set the right vision, people will make the right decisions, and you'll be successful.

Adding Value to the Company

I add value to the company by choosing the right people to lead the organization. Health care organizations are very complex. Therefore, selecting the right people to lead key functional areas is a significant undertaking. If you get the right people in place, your chances of success are much better.

The other way I add value is simply by making decisions. It's easy to get bogged down in bureaucracy in this industry. There are many things that are beyond your control, so your ability to impact change can easily stagnate. Don't shoot from the hip, but make decisions and prioritize. We have thirty things that are important to do, so how do we prioritize limited resources to get something accomplished? It's easy to get completely lost in the effort of balancing things to meet society's aims, and at the same time making money and staying in business. That's where effective, informed decision making can make a huge difference. I add value just by keeping the focus on getting things done. If you focus on the right things and do them correctly, you'll be financially solvent.

Qualities for Success

As a CEO, you have to be approachable. Even though I am the president and CEO, most employees would feel very comfortable calling me by my first name. When I'm wandering around at one of our hospitals or other entities, it's important to be able to interact with employees and show them I'm interested in what they're doing. I like to put what they're doing in the context of the overall success of the business, so they understand why their roles are important.

In this day and age, you have to have a tremendous sense of integrity. Regardless of what industry you're in, you must have a strong sense of integrity and be able to articulate that. Also, you have to be inquisitive and ask questions. When you show interest, people want to talk to you; they are interested in explaining what they do.

Last but not least, there are times when you have to be tough. You have to be able to make tough, sometimes unpopular decisions, and be comfortable with them. Health care is no different than any other industry in that regard. It's not easy to fire people, but sometimes you have to, and you have to be able to say no. We have a unique environment in this industry with the relationship between hospitals, physicians, patients, and staff.

Strategies for the Health Care Industry

We're dealing with human lives in our industry. If there's a glitch in a furniture company and a chair doesn't get made, it's not a societal issue. In health care, we're dealing with people's health and well-being. If we don't have the right people or processes in place, the impact of doing something negative to a human life is significant. We have a real sense of social responsibility. We're dealing with something incredibly precious, and people are often coming to us during a very stressful or traumatic time in their lives, which dramatically impacts our interaction with them.

Health care organizations are very intense environments, and employees and patients are under a great deal of stress. As a leader in this type of organization, you have to be careful not to overreact when hearing one side of a story. I always try to listen to both sides of the issue. The other thing we are careful to do at Spectrum Health is to not defer tough decisions. Sometimes, deferring decisions may be the right strategy, but doing it just for the sake of escaping responsibility is a bad policy, and we discourage it. My management style is such that I need to be surrounded by good people, and I have high expectations. Track records speak for themselves—if you have a solid track record, you have ample opportunities to be successful.

Top Industry Challenges

In health care, the main challenge is dealing with constant change. You have to be incredibly flexible. The reimbursement mechanism in health care is so different than in any other industry. There are government programs such as Medicaid and Medicare, as well as private third-party insurers. It's probably one of the most complicated systems for providing and being paid for services. The government payment programs are part of the entire fabric of our economy. Things are always changing, which makes it difficult to plan for the long term, even though we attempt to do so. Having a vision and a strategic plan that goes out five to ten years is critical.

Another major challenge, on a personal basis, is the balance between work and home. I have really tried to make my family a high priority, even though it isn't always easy. Doing your best to maintain that balance makes you a better person in the long run, and it sensitizes you to your employees.

Getting the right people in the right places is challenging. We have a hiring process we call the "behavior method" of hiring. It's based around how you fit into the organizational culture, and how you make decisions. The other thing we do is manage change. It's difficult to gauge how much change an organization will accept. We have so many things going on—our organization could be in constant turmoil if we're not careful. I must be able to balance what needs to change to move forward with what needs to stay the same to lend stability to the organization. That's a very difficult balance.

It's also a challenge to manage the expectations of the community we serve, and of the people who work here. How do you measure these expectations and, more importantly, how do you make sure you don't overreach or have unreasonable expectations? One misconception people have about my position is that I always have all the data I need to make decisions. Many times, as CEO, you need to be comfortable making decisions with less than 100 percent of the information at your fingertips. People assume you're always going to be right because you have all the information in front of you. There is a general lack of understanding of what it takes to make those decisions, and the time it takes to come to key decisions.

Working with Other Executives

I work most closely with the chief financial officer (CFO), the chief operating officer (COO), and business development (marketing and planning). A vast majority of my time is spent with the board of directors. When it comes to the other executives on our team, I have to understand enough about their positions to ask the right kinds of questions. I don't profess to know as much in finance as our CFO, but I need to know enough to understand how finances fit into our overall strategy. In return, they need to share in my vision, understand it, and agree with it. If members in key positions are on board, things get done.

I look for executives who are good athletes, meaning people who can do many things. They're smart, flexible, big-picture thinkers, and multifaceted. They need to be results-oriented people with good sensibility and balance. I look for people who can keep things in perspective. This is such a changing environment—if you have people who are limited in their abilities, they're not going to make it. That's also how you weed people out: when the world changes around them, they have to be able to adapt.

When tracking the progress of my fellow executives, I consider where we are in relation to our:

- Vision
- Strategic plan
- Five-year financial plan

We connect these metrics into performance pay. There are checks and balances that tie compensation on an annualized basis to the individual goals of each executive. That's one way I determine how successful they are. It starts from the vision and extends to the strategic plan and the financial plan.

Executive Advice

The most common advice I give to my executives is simply to calm down. Better decisions are made with a clear head. This is a stressful place at times, and the calming influence of the CEO is critical. It's the CEO's job to emphasize that if you just relax for a moment, you'll make a better decision.

I had a mentor who once told me that you don't have to win every battle. There are going to be times when the better decision is to let someone else win, and move on to the next battle. This is especially true in a health care environment, where you have a lot of physician interaction. If you're combative and focused only on winning, to the point that it separates you from someone else, it'll wear you and the organization down. You can't always be in conflict.

Working with Physicians

One of my key personal strategies revolves around working with physicians. I am always looking for ways in which we can incorporate a group as significant as the medical staff into our long-term strategic plan. I'm working to develop a culture where physicians are integral to all of our services. We have created several joint ventures related to diagnostic, service, or radiology centers. Working with physicians has been an instrumental part of our success.

Sometimes, you have to give something up in order to get something long-term. If you take a short-term view of everything, you'll never do anything with anybody, because you'll want to keep the environment the way it is; that's unrealistic amidst all of today's changes. You have to be willing to trade off a few things in order to make a connection with physicians for long-term benefit.

Biggest Expenses

Bricks and mortar are our greatest expense and our biggest risk. Health care is changing, and we need to be sure the demand for our services will sustain the need for our buildings. As technology advances, there is always the possibility that procedures can be done outside of the traditional hospital setting. For example, if we build a heart center and then procedures become available that eliminate the need for the center, we suffer the consequences.

The other big expense for us is people. Health care is very labor-intensive, so 55 to 60 percent of our expenses revolve around labor. At the executive level, the big expense is research and development (R&D). What guides us when we're looking at expenses is our value proposition. To us, value means high quality, low cost. If we can do something that provides that kind of value, it's going to be successful.

R&D and Top Resources

At Spectrum Health, we make R&D a priority. We have specialists on our staff, and we use outside consultants as well. We track new technology and look for what is on the horizon. We have contracts with outside organizations that are on the cutting edge of technology trends, as are many of our in-house people. Continuing education is critical to this area, so that our teams are constantly acquiring new information and are aware of trends related to the health care field. R&D is always a key topic at our executive retreats; we dedicate considerable resources in terms of funding and people to this effort.

As a CEO, the most important resource for me is reading material. I like to read things that aren't health care-related, and have applications in other industries. For too long, health care has viewed itself as an isolated industry—it has imagined that nothing that works in any other industry could work here. But the more we know about what's working in other industries, the better off we will be.

Another key resource for me is my past experience: lessons learned from other organizations I've been involved with. It's always helpful to reflect on what I tried in other places, and what worked and what didn't work. Sometimes it's environment-specific, but most of the time it has a fundamental component to it. It's about drawing on the experience I've gained over the years.

The Changing Role of the CEO

I believe CEOs do a lot more coaching now than they used to, but at the same time it's harder to be visible to employees. We have 13,000 staff members and 140 service sites across western Michigan. As CEO, I have to combine the vision of where we want to go in the long term with making sure we're operating from day to day and taking care of patients. You can spend all your time on an elaborate vision, but if your product is no good, it doesn't matter. You have to be focused simultaneously on the present and the future, with one foot in each camp.

In the coming years, having core knowledge about the operations side of things will be increasingly important. In health care, it's going to be about results and transparency. The key is going to be making sure decisions are made transparent to the community, the board, and employees. There are very few secrets in health care anyway, but I think there will be fewer in the years ahead.

Amid all these changes, there are three things that will distinguish successful CEOs. First, the best CEOs never underestimate the intelligence of their employees. At Spectrum Health, we have a wide variety of people working in very distinct areas who all have different levels of experience. It's important never to underestimate their intelligence or their ability to make significant contributions. Second, successful CEOs evaluate the political environment and make decisions with that in mind. This requires understanding what has to be done today, and knowing how that impacts what needs to get done tomorrow. Finally, smart CEOs surround themselves with the best people and listen to them. This approach will lead to a much better chance of survival and success. This industry is so complex; I would never sleep at night if I were the only one expected to have all the answers.

Richard C. Breon, an industry veteran with more than twenty-eight years of health care administration experience, has been president and chief executive officer of Spectrum Health since 2000.

At Spectrum Health, Mr. Breon is responsible for the vision and strategic oversight of western Michigan's largest health system. Spectrum Health has more than 13,000 employees and $2.3 billion in revenue. The system's 1,400 affiliated medical staff provides care to patients at more than 140 service locations. In addition, the health care system includes a 450,000-member managed care plan, helicopter transport service, long-term and continuing care services, home care, and hospice care. Spectrum Health has earned more than thirty national awards during the past five years, including being named among the Solucient "100 Top Hospitals" and "Top Integrated Healthcare Networks," and being included in U.S. News & World Report*'s list of "America's Best Hospitals."*

Prior to joining Spectrum Health, Mr. Breon was president and chief executive officer for Mission Health System, Inc., in Evansville, Indiana, a member of Ascension Health, the largest not-for-profit health care system in the country. While at Mission Health System, Mr. Breon developed Genesis Health Alliance, a managed care network linking fourteen rural hospitals, and successfully negotiated the acquisition of a competing 350-bed facility with revenues of $120 million.

Previously, he served as president and chief executive officer of St. Mary's Medical Center in Evansville and Mercy Hospital in Iowa City. He also held senior management positions at Brackenridge Hospital in Austin, Texas, and Iowa Methodist Medical Center in Des Moines, Iowa.

Mr. Breon earned a bachelor's degree from Iowa State University and a master's degree in hospital and health administration from the University of Iowa.

In 2003, Mr. Breon was one of just six health care professionals in the state of Michigan appointed by Governor Jennifer Granholm to the state's Certificate of Need Commission. He also was appointed by former Governor John Engler in 2002 to serve on the state's Hospital Advisory Commission.

Mr. Breon has held many civic- and health care-related board positions throughout his career. He is currently a board member for the Michigan Hospital Association, the Alliance for Health, and the Right Place. He is also a fellow of the American College of Healthcare Executives.

An Academic Point of View

Gordon Gee

Chancellor

Vanderbilt University

My Goals

I am the chancellor at Vanderbilt University. The role of a chancellor or president at an educational institution is one of strong and consistent leadership rather than management. People in my position have the opportunity to paint a vision and set a strategy for the university. We are fortunate to have the chance to nurture people by engaging in their strategy and believing in their vision. Ultimately, my work is about being able to garner the resources and leadership necessary to make the school's overarching vision a reality. The university setting is increasingly complex, so I need a focused agenda at all times. At the very beginning of my presidency at Vanderbilt, I set out five focused yet overarching goals that our efforts to meet would result in the transformation of this university: we would renew our commitment to the undergraduate experience at Vanderbilt; we would reinvent graduate education here; we would reintegrate our professional schools with the intellectual life of the university; we would reexamine and consequently restructure our economic models; and we would renew Vanderbilt's covenant with the community that supports us.

I continue, as this university continues, to revisit those goals all the time, to see how we are progressing in relation to them, and also to see if a certain policy decision supports and promotes them. This practice results in a certain economy of line; we tend not to involve ourselves in reforms or efforts that are not in service of one or more of those goals.

Creating Financial Impact

There are some critical initiatives that help me create financial impact and add value to the university. The first of these initiatives is to set specific goals and create sound strategies. I recruit faculty members and students who add a tremendous value to the university. If we have smart people teaching smart people, the value of our institution will be greatly enhanced.

Educational institutions are complex financial machines. I need to make sure we have a strategy in place for managing our financial resources in order to enhance the quality of the institution. When this happens, people will be willing to invest further. We do not produce products, but we do trade ideas. If we are creating better ideas than anyone else out there, people will be willing to invest in us. This adds both intellectual and financial value.

Universities are people-intensive. The biggest expense we incur is our personnel cost. Our personnel expenses generally comprise about 75 to 85 percent of the overall cost of the university. When we have additional money in the budget, we go through a prioritization process. It is all part of our five-year strategic view of the institution. We are constantly prioritizing and determining how initiatives fit into the long-range issues we have to confront.

The Art of Being a Chancellor

There is a definite art to being a chancellor at an educational institution. A chancellor must first and foremost have a good sense of humor, not only because humor relaxes a rather intense atmosphere and makes your colleagues feel positively about the work they do, but also because not taking yourself too seriously allows you to be more adaptive and resilient, more flexible in what you are willing to hear from others. But under that softness, you have to have a steely quality, for the same reason. It is also important to have thick skin and nerves of steel in this position, because a university community comprises so many differently vested interests, that there is always someone who will not be entirely happy with a decision you have made, and will criticize it strongly. You cannot allow yourself to be stampeded or overrun by criticism. Humor helps you survive it, but a dedication to the good of the university community over the long term will help you have the resolve you need to uphold your decision. I have to be willing to make hard decisions and stick with them.

There have been a number of successful chancellors and presidents with vastly different personalities. For me, success has been achieved through the practices of listening, leadership, and cooperating. One cannot be a good leader without first learning how to be a good follower.

Chancellors must listen very carefully to the people they serve. These people include faculty members, students, and the president, people, and state at a public university. The willingness to make hard decisions, even when they contradict what everyone else thinks, is important in this job. A certain "ingrained-ed-ness" can occur at universities, because in addition to being places of innovation, they are also places of dearly observed tradition—even if that tradition is just one of habit. When I combined the office of provost with the office of vice chancellor for development and alumni relations, in order that our fundraising would be in alignment with and support our strategic academic goals, I received much resistance—but I was never able to discern a deeper rationale than "We've never done it that way." But now we have a fundraising process that is much more streamlined and strategically canny.

Unique Aspects of Higher Education

There are some unique aspects of working in higher education. Even though we are a very large, $2 billion organization, we are not actually a business. We do not think of ourselves as a business, and we do not act like a business. We are not driven by quarterly reports or bottom lines. We are driven by excellence.

Our world is one of discovery. We are constantly trying to nurture the next big idea and make sure new and innovative methods of thought are welcomed on our campus. We have placed an especial emphasis on combining faculty members from different disciplines, making them and their work more available to one another in order to give a chance to what results from the intellectual mixing. We hire innovators. And we are absolute defenders of academic freedom.

Strategies for Success

The art of listening is enormously important in my position. I bring an open mind and a willing ear to this job. I try to develop a clear vision for the institution, and I state it clearly. I give people the chance to agree or disagree with my vision. If I do not hear too much disagreement, we will move down my intended path.

Universities have a strange organizational structure. Most of our leadership initiatives happen through collaborative conversation and persuasion. We have to make people understand what we are trying to do, and then sell that vision continuously. Even though universities are not supposed to be political organizations, they are precisely that. Universities are the most non-political political organizations on earth. Selling our ideas and moving our agenda through the art of persuasion are solid campaign strategies that lead to success.

Vanderbilt is trying to grow in quality. Our strategy is to make certain we do what we do better than anyone else. We are constantly looking for talent. Our focus is the acquisition and retention of talent, as well as the creation of new and interesting programs that will differentiate us from other institutions.

Universities are all about research and development. We do $400 million worth of research every year. We are in the idea business, so research and development are not strategies for us—they are the entire reason we exist. I love creativity and finding ways to do things better.

I find human resources to be the most interesting part of what I do. The creative minds of the faculty and students, and the ways they generate ideas and opportunities within the institution, are inspiring. The external resources available to our university, including the support of the friends and alumni who give generously, make a huge difference to the institution.

Challenging Aspects of Being a Chancellor

I live in a world of infinite appetites and finite resources, and I often refer to the university as an ecosystem in order to illustrate this. A university does not have an endless expanse of capital from which to draw, but it does support so many varied interests—I would call them niches—that just in themselves could make endless claims upon that central resource. They all have to be supported to the degree to which we can support them, but their interests have to be held in balance with all others at the university.

Everyone believes his or her division is the most central to the success of the university. Very often, a university views itself as a confederation of colleges and departments instead of as one central ecological system. The way I go about making someone understand that the ecology of the university is more important than his or her particular program is always a large challenge for me. If an individual program does well, it adds value to our ecology and sociology, but it is not always the central reason we exist.

It is always difficult to choose between solid ideas. It is very easy to say no when there is a bad idea or issue. The challenge occurs when there are promising ideas and I am not able to support them because of finite resources. I hate to see good ideas go to waste. I handle these situations as expeditiously as I can. I apologize but try to be encouraging by saying that this is not the last time the idea will be considered. I try to revisit it when we have dealt with some of our higher priorities.

One of the biggest misconceptions about my position is that the university chancellor is all-powerful. The truth is that the most powerful people in a university are the faculty and the students. The university chancellor is in a position to muster resources to support faculty and students, but I have to listen to the constituents. If I fall out of step without developing leadership strategy, I will find myself incapable of leading without community support.

The Team

I work closely with my six vice chancellors. There is the vice chancellor for administration, the vice chancellor for public affairs, the vice chancellor for student life and university affairs, the vice chancellor for investments, and the two chief academic officers—the provost, who runs all academic activities, and the vice chancellor for health affairs, who runs our vast medical center.

The command and control system, where the chancellor makes the decisions and the vice chancellors and dean are simply seen as staff officers, does not work. I believe the success of this university lies in our cooperative spirit. I tell my vice chancellors that first they are university officers. This means they have to understand all aspects of the university. They also have to be supportive of what is happening across the institution by advocating for their particular portfolio.

In a team member, I look for different skills depending on the position. I want people who are bright and creative. I need people who are constantly looking for new and innovative solutions to problems. I want people who understand the values of the university and the unique nature of the institution.

I have a goal-setting process for the team. I send out a note to team members and ask them for their top five goals for the year. I also ask them to explain how they accomplished their goals from the past year, and how their goals line up with the general goals of the university. Then I share my goals with them. I try to keep goals limited to five, because I believe it is impossible to accomplish more than five major initiatives in a given goal-setting period.

I ask my team members to always stay focused on what they are doing. The purpose for us as an institution is to focus and execute. I remind people that we are all about talent at this university. We constantly have to be seeking, nurturing, and creating new opportunity for talent within the institution.

I once received a piece of advice I thought was wrong. A very prominent president of a university told me I should not be too engaged in the institution, because it will never love me back. I do not buy that. On the flip side, the best piece of advice I ever received is to be passionate about what I am doing. I do not do this as a job. I view it as a calling and an opportunity.

The Changing Role of the Chancellor

I have been a university president for twenty-five years, and my role has changed drastically. The world we live in now is dramatically different than it was when I first became a university president. Much of this comes from the fact that we live in a smaller world, one driven by technology and concerned about external threats. This has an impact on the business of education.

In this small world where instant messaging occurs, the Internet is the way to communicate broadly. We can get instant response. That kind of technology has changed the nature of universities in terms of what we do and how we communicate, not only by facilitating communication across the body of the "company" (making sure all faculty and staff are involved with the current life of the institution), but also by internationalizing the work of universities by sustaining us in constant contact with our colleagues and peers in other institutions all over the world.

In the coming years, leadership duties for university presidents will remain the same, although the issues we deal with will be different. I do not expect the role to change as much as the issues. We have to constantly reinvent ourselves in this role. There are certain patterns of intuitiveness to listening, leadership, modes of inquiry, and communication that are important. Ultimately, the nature of leadership will remain steady even as the nature of the institution changes.

Chancellor Gordon Gee leads Vanderbilt University with a commitment to a quest for talent as the institution further advances its mission of creating a culture of simplicity, clarity, agility, and accountability. With an added emphasis on clarity and execution, it is clear that the institution's strategic investment in areas such as recruitment and retention of faculty, increasing affordability for students, and the transformation of graduate education have strengthened the character of Vanderbilt and propel the university even further into the ranks of the world's finest institutions of higher education. And, Mr. Gee continues to place special emphasis on increasing Vanderbilt's commitment to and participation within the community, specifically through the development and enhancement of world-class scholarship, teaching, public service, and patient care.

Deeply involved with Nashville and middle Tennessee, Mr. Gee helps conduct Circle of Hope, a philanthropic leadership program organized by the Tennessee chapter of the Cystic Fibrosis Foundation, and serves on the Nashville Symphony Association's board of directors, as well as the board of directors of the Freedom Forum Diversity Institute, Inc., and he is a member of the advisory committee for the Nashville Alliance for Public Education. He is also a member of the board of directors for Nashville's Montgomery Bell Academy and the board of the Tennessee College Association. In conjunction with Vanderbilt, Mr. Gee was awarded the Outstanding Promotion of Diversity Award by the Nashville branch of the NAACP.

Mr. Gee is part of the College Board's Commission on Writing in America's Schools and Colleges, an advisory committee of nationally recognized experts who will help develop the new SAT exam, as well as the steering committee for a new National Center for Public Policy and Higher Education. He currently serves as a director or trustee of the

Jason Foundation, the Freedom Forum Diversity Institute, the National Hospice Foundation, the historic black college and university advisory committee of the Kresge Foundation, the Campus Compact, Dollar General Corporation, Massey Energy Corporation, and Gaylord Entertainment Company. Additionally, he is a member of the President's Council for Imagining America: Artists and Scholars in Public Life, the Association of Governing Boards of Universities and Colleges Advisory Council of Presidents, the Christopher Isherwood Foundation Board, and the Business-Higher Education Forum.

One of the most experienced chief executives in higher education, Mr. Gee previously served as president of Brown University, Ohio State University, the University of Colorado, and West Virginia University. A joint degree recipient in law and education from Columbia University, Mr. Gee completed a federal judicial clerkship, after which he served as an assistant dean for the University of Utah College of Law. After holding this position, Mr. Gee served as a judicial fellow and senior staff assistant for United States Supreme Court Chief Justice Warren Burger. He then became associate dean and professor at J. Reuben Clark Law School of Brigham Young University, and next served as dean at West Virginia University. It was at West Virginia University that he made the transition from law school administrator to university president.

Mr. Gee has been a trustee for the Harry S. Truman Scholarship Foundation since 1995. He has carried out research on behalf of the Ford Foundation, the Guy Anderson Foundation, and the American Bar Foundation, among others. He is the co-author of six books, and the author of numerous papers and articles in fields relating to both law and education. The recipient of a number of awards and honors, he was a Mellon fellow for the Aspen Institute for Humanistic Studies and a W.K. Kellogg fellow. In 1994, he received the Distinguished Alumnus Award from the University of Utah, and in 1994 he received the same award from the Teachers College at Columbia University.

The father of Rebekah, he is married to Constance, an associate professor of public policy and education at Peabody College, Vanderbilt University.

Creating Sustainable Value as a CEO in the Manufacturing Industry

Harold Bevis

Chief Executive Officer, President, and Director

Pliant Corporation

Manufacturing Success

To successfully lead a profitable manufacturing company, you must have a defined value proposition backed up by people, plans, and processes to deliver it–by doing so, you will always come out on top. How to determine the right answer for your company? The answer always varies. For example, a company with a business base that has a low frequency of product change (say once a year) and relatively high volumes per SKU will gravitate to low-cost countries (China/Asia Pacific, India, Central Europe) as their home base. Industries with a higher frequency of innovation (say three times per year) will stay closer to the local market they're serving, as being quick-reacting is a bigger part of the business model and the best way to make money—versus a slower reacting but lower-cost supply chain from China. The best manufacturing companies deeply understand their business models at a DNA level, benchmark their business models against primary competitors, stay even with their peer group on operating efficiencies, and surpass them in innovation around core product performance, product package, total cost, and services offerings. In my opinion, the companies that are the most innovative in these areas win the battle.

Our company is part of a fairly mature industry, plastic packaging, but there are many different approaches to this market. We focus heavily on our core products; we don't try to be a one-stop shop for all customers. Instead, we tell customers that we can help them subdivide their purchasing so they control their costs and simplify their solutions.

Our customers tell us they like working with us because we are open-minded about bringing in other companies if we feel we don't have the right answer. We believe that if we honestly, diligently, and transparently look out for our customers' best interests, they will favor us when their needs *do* fall into our strike zone.

In short, there are three very important tenets to achieving manufacturing success:

Pick the best people to lead your company. No business plan or long-term strategic plan has a preordained right to happen. You must have the best possible people in key jobs to deal with the "stuff happens" factor and pounce on unforeseen opportunities when they happen. In my experience, you can never have enough cunning sales leaders or angry engineers. They will win a lot of battles.

Align your company with the most creative customers. There is a reason why certain companies stay on top of their industries for a long time—companies like Cisco Systems, IBM, 3M, and Proctor & Gamble. My experience has been that if you can satisfy the most discriminating winner, a lot of great business practices are created and standardized within your own company. Just like a super leader will bring out the best in others, a super customer will bring out the best in the company.

Focus on your core strengths and strive to improve them. No company can be everything to everyone. This is an ever-present temptation. Stick to the company's core profitable products and be the best at delivering those year after year after year.

Growing Revenues and Profits

Revenue growth requires a multilayered business strategy that integrates plans for product innovation, plant/process innovation, customer relationship building, and key marketing events. We set appropriate growth targets for each business unit based on its opportunity set and how much we want to bet on that business unit. I am a momentum investor in this regard. Even if a business unit has a seemingly attractive growth program, I may pass on it if that business team has not been delivering. Growth is hard work, and you need to bet on teams that get the job done. We do set explicit growth targets, and the people are measured on achieving their annual goals. Product development programs are created in an iterative way by creating the largest possible opportunity set to choose from, selecting the set we believe is the right short-term and long-term call for our company, and then creating an annual execution plan that we measure. Engineering takes the lead, and we measure project implementation. In addition, we invest in several large research and development projects every year that help us to develop new ideas and stay competitive within the industry over the longer term.

We also try to drive down our manufacturing fixed costs in the plants and warehouses, and we develop business process improvement plans that can help us save money with the right amount of spending. Many of these plans focus on waste elimination and lean manufacturing, which is something we always need to monitor closely. We analyze gross waste, net waste, customer quality waste, return waste, over-spec waste, and setup waste.

We also try to drive down our central corporate costs—finance, human resources, legal, information technology, and medical benefits. Our human resource strategy is to have the best possible person in every job; we believe that doing so leads to lower overall payroll costs over the long term. This is sort of an oxymoron—we try to pay our people very well, but we tend to have fewer people. We look to implement ideas such as systematizing customer service in order to minimize headcount. Like most other companies, we look closely at medical coverage costs, but we also take a very creative approach to health coverage that includes employee wellness programs, and that can result in fewer medical claims.

Twice a year, we analyze customer profitability and product mix. It's important to be aware of profit trends in customer and product categories so corrective action can be taken if needed. These are largely creeping issues that need to be monitored. Materials costs are also very important. You want to use the right materials that lead to the lowest possible waste and the highest amount of sellable product per pound of input material.

Competing in the Market

Retail and wholesale markets have different requirements. In regard to retail, Proctor & Gamble talks about the "First Moment of Truth" and the "Second Moment of Truth." The first moment is: Will the shopper in the store (they are not a consumer yet—just a shopper) reach out and take your product off of the shelf? The packaging is essential in winning the shelf battle. The second moment is: When the consumer (the person is now a consumer, since the purchase has been made) uses the product, does he or she like it, and does it meet their expectations? If so, they will likely buy it again and develop brand loyalty. If they don't like it, they may try something else next time.

There is a corollary between these retail moments of truth and wholesale products as well. The first value test is whether the customer decides to procure your product based on initial trials, evaluations, price, and terms and conditions. The second value test pertains to supply chain performance: Does the product consistently get to where it is supposed to go, on time, with no damage or paperwork errors? A third value test can also be applied to account value creation. You need to look at whether the company consistently brings forward-thinking ideas to the customer that will help them improve their business. If you pass these three tests, you will consistently beat the competition in the wholesale arena.

Products and Profit

For most manufacturers in process industries, raw materials are the number-one cost, followed by equipment depreciation/amortization, overhead, and labor costs. Raw materials are also the number-one cost for manufacturers focused on assembly, but labor is their second most significant cost, followed by overhead and depreciation/amortization. Raw materials have become exceedingly important as China has risen to power in the world's workshop. They are a huge global buyer of these materials, and their actions ripple into raw material markets worldwide—steel, paper, aluminum, plastics, and coal. Raw material strategies have become a top-shelf strategic issue for today's manufacturing chief executive officers, versus relegation to a procurement person. This is a new and challenging dynamic. Today's successful manufacturing company will have very smart, technically sound leader in charge of raw materials.

The best profit scenario for any manufacturing company is when you have a product that is the leader in its category, has a compelling price/value perceptive, resonates with customers' core values, is backed up and protected by patents and intellectual property safeguards, and has great profit and growth rates. When all of these conditions are met, you have a home run. However, these are hard to come by. But they are the goal of every manufacturing company with a fire in its belly.

The more typical great profit scenario is one that involves a niche or specialized product that makes great money for a certain application that has limited competition. Or a scenario where a customer buys the best stuff—a high-profit product mix. Low-profit commodity products are not bad. They pay the bills, and you can use them to pull through a profitable mix at an account or penetrate a winning customer.

Worst case scenarios are ones where you are just selling a low-profit product to a customer that does not or can not buy any of your profitable products. This scenario is destined for a low profit forever. If you choose to stay with these accounts, the goal is to keep all costs as low as possible—including variable selling costs like sales commissions, rebate programs, and cash discounts.

Making Sure the Company Stays on Target

There are several steps you can take to ensure that your company stays on target.

1. Make sure you have leaders who understand the company's game plan over the short and long term.
2. Make sure your key leaders have the DNA to get you where you want to go.
3. Have a well thought out plan based on real trends and real actions.
4. Put in place incentive plans based on achievement of plan objectives. Vary incentive compensation significantly so people see that great performance will put a lot of money in your pocket and get you promoted.
5. Always invest for the second year with half of the current year's money.
6. Invest some money from the current year into the third year.
7. Measure performance-to-plan on a monthly basis and be tough enough to make corrective actions when you need to, even if no other person agrees with you.
8. Deal with underperformers bluntly and decisively.
9. Ride your top performers and be a momentum investor—top-performing plants, people, and products.
10. Always have fun and take time to visibly recognize great performances.

In terms of financial success, you want to meet the current year goals as well as the three-year goals. Financially, you don't ever want to go backwards. You know you have achieved customer success when you have the most admired customers in the industry; and you win awards from them. You know you have achieved employee success when you can truthfully say that you provide fair compensation, that you help employees grow professionally, and that you provide them with advancement options when they are deserved.

Industry Changes

Many changes have occurred in manufacturing during the past several years. The raw material industry has consolidated significantly, giving companies a great deal of pricing power. In the future, we will see more raw material supplies available online in the Middle East and Asia, which will enable the local markets to thrive.

We've also seen the larger retailers and grocers gain a tremendous amount of power due to the decreasing power of brands. In 1980, you could reach 80 percent of United States households with a television add on three stations. Today, that same feat requires simultaneous advertising on more than 110 channels. And that is before the advent of TiVo. Many of the large consumer products companies believe their products must do a lot of the talking for them, since they cannot create brand image and brand preference through the mass media effectively anymore.

Packaging is more important than ever in this new reality. Those who have the most innovative packaging will stand out in the market and, ultimately, win the market.

To keep up with changes and to make sure we address our customers' changing needs, we take a multi-pronged approach. For example, we invest time and money in truly getting to know what is happening with our large customers. We have technical seminars, private innovation discussions/displays, and co-developments around research and development programs. In this way, we can informally interact with them, hear what they have to say about whether or not they are happy with our product offerings and innovation direction, and find out what they think about our competitors. Having dedicated teams for large accounts is also very important. We make sure large accounts receive the very highest level of service and commitment from our company.

We also participate in major industry trade shows; this increases our awareness of what is going on in the industry, and provides additional opportunities to meet customers. It's also a good idea to speak at industry events so you have a public presence and force yourself to have clear thoughts.

To keep up with technology changes, we regularly meet with raw material suppliers and equipment vendors. Maintaining an active research and development program can also help you stay current, especially in your core areas.

Understanding Your Competition

To outperform your competition, you need to first understand your competition. Review the latest market data. Read all you can about your key competitors. Know who you are up against. When you have access to all of this information, you can aggressively protect your market position. Never forget that competing in any market is a zero-sum game.

But it takes more than just knowing your competitors if you want to be successful. You need to have a compelling value proposition that matters to the customer. In any industry, customers look for aggressive, proactive partners; they want to be working with a company that won't miss out on the next best thing.

The face of competition is changing. For example, China is a powerhouse now; we have unimpeded free trade with them. It's important that companies understand how they can leverage China's inherent strengths and advantages and/or play off of them. China is a big and powerful factor in manufacturing companies today.

The Internet has significantly impacted competition as well. The global marketplace is much easier to access, and online buying has become much more commonplace. The Internet has increased convenience, but it has decreased the bonds of long-term partnerships and relationships.

Industry Benchmarking

Financial metrics are a good way to measure how your company is doing in comparison to the competition, but you also need to understand why—and in what areas—your successes and failures have occurred. It's a great idea to hire people from the competition every now and then. You can also gain insight into how your company is doing by listening to why customers like you—and why they don't. Find out why customers like the competitors—and why they don't. People, projects, timing, and numbers: they all need to be considered when you are benchmarking the competition and looking to make adjustments within your company accordingly.

To stay ahead of the competition, you need to be looking always at your bottom line performance on long-term growth and long-term profit rate vis-à-vis your industry. You need to have a value proposition your competition doesn't have; one that matters to customers. And you need to always remember how important innovation is—it can help you move forward in the market and move ahead of your competition.

Building Customer Relationships and Loyalty

Unfortunately, in today's world loyalty is at a minimum, and at a premium. Everyone needs to be aware of that, which means satisfying your customer's ongoing needs is of paramount importance. More than ever, it's essential that you think creatively and proactively about your business and how to seemingly integrate it into your customer's business model.

Steady, excellent performance in terms of products and services is essential if you want customer loyalty. In addition, you need to be diligent about building personal relationships with your customers, mainly by tackling tough tasks for your customers and solving them.

When all is said and done, you need to be the best provider of your core products—no matter what. Simply put, you cannot run and hide from that reality—it's the very essence of successful manufacturing.

Harold Bevis has devoted his career to turning around underperforming midsized manufacturing companies. As chief executive officer of Plaint Corporation, he is now working in his third turnaround, the second as chief executive officer. Previously, he served as group president and corporate officer of Emerson Electric Company and as chief executive officer, president, and board member of Jordan Telecommunication Products.

Each of these companies involved over $1 billion of capital. Well versed in the world of high finance and leveraged buyouts, Mr. Bevis typically teams up with private equity firms, investment banks, and commercial banks. His role as the chief executive officer is to assess the company's difficulties, develop a sustainable winning game plan, rally the team, and top-grade where necessary. When the capital markets are right, he then converts that value into profit for the owners. Always a stakeholder himself in the companies he turns around, he is currently one of the largest individual stockholders of Pliant Corporation.

In his first year at Pliant, Mr. Bevis has overseen the first organic sales growth the company has seen in six years, an increase of EBITDA by 10 percent over the previous year, as well as nearly a 50 percent turnover of top executives.

Previously, Mr. Bevis served as senior vice president and general manager at General Cable Corporation, where he joined a buyout/turnaround team led by a former General Electric executive.

A Three-Word Job: Vision, Talent, and Environment

Daniel J. Roselli
President
Red F Marketing

The Job Description of a CEO

At the chief executive officer (CEO) level, the job description can be summarized in three words: vision, talent, and environment. A CEO uses these three words to drive business every day. With vision, a CEO must set a compelling, meaningful, and motivating vision for the team, communicate that vision effectively, and ensure that a team understands the vision. The idea of talent involves getting, keeping, and growing the best talent. The integral component of any successful company is having the best employees and the companies with the best talent win—period. The third concept is environment; it involves creating an environment in which the right vision and the right team can flourish. In the end, a good leader should have accomplished those three components.

Maintaining the culture of the company is also a part of the job of a CEO. It is important to keep the core elements of the culture of a small company, even though the company continues to grow. A CEO must constantly adjust his or her management leadership styles and practices as the company grows, changes, and becomes more successful. In doing so, a CEO must remain focused on what the company is trying to achieve. I use the analogy of a lighthouse that always has a fixed beacon for a company and its employees to reference.

An Art Form

The art of being a CEO rests in two capabilities—balancing a numbers orientation with a people orientation, as well as possessing a fluid, adaptable leadership style. Successful CEOs understand how to drive their business forward analytically, but they also have a sense of self-confidence, charisma, and leadership. He or she must be a balance between a financial, number-driven orientation and a more managerial, people-driven orientation. He or she must be analytically driven with the ability to assess key variables and the initiatives to drive the business forward. The other side involves dealing with people, culture, and positioning. Leaders should be able to switch between them easily.

Everyone also has a default leadership style they feel the most comfortable using. Some individuals can switch from being effective doers to effective managers if they become good with a particular style, whether it is dictatorial, democratic, or consensus-building. A CEO truly becomes effective when he or she changes between the various leadership styles in order to adapt and make an impact in different situations.

Team Members

Our firm generally hires based on two characteristics—intellect and enthusiasm—because those are the two traits that cannot be taught. As a result of hiring bright talent, these companies do not need massive process and regulations, but instead individuals create their own processes. This lack of structure also helps maintain the fast response and change nature that is so valued in the marketing industry. One characteristic we place less value on is years and years of industry experience. Instead, marketing firms understand that bright individuals will learn, adapt, and change according to the situation in which they are placed.

In order to maximize growth and set goals for team members, a company should plan from the ground up versus from the top down. After discussing some overall objectives for the company, individual employees are then asked to set goals in line with those objectives. As a result, employees can take ownership of their goals. All individuals should have a documented performance plan and a documented individual development plan for the year so they know the exact tasks they need to accomplish. Once these goals are established, the best piece of advice I give my team members is to focus. Even though twenty issues combine to create an overall project, an individual must focus on his or her part in the scheme in order for the team to be successful.

Performance plans should be reviewed informally every quarter, and more formally every six months. At the end of the year, a company should review whether or not it met objectives by having a more formal year-end performance evaluation. By having multiple informal and formal reviews, a company can stress that setting goals is an ongoing daily process.

The Role of Management

At a small entrepreneurial company like Red F, we strive to have no levels of management; instead, every employee reports directly to an individual on the management team. I believe layers are exponentially bureaucratic rather than linearly bureaucratic. As a result, I work with all the employees at the company. Because of this structure, it is important for all employees to rally behind and understand the vision of the company. Everyone must also know how their job contributes to that vision.

As a result, I meet with the management team one hour every week. At this meeting, the agenda rotates each week among the various topics the management team must cover, including operations, personnel, business development, and client development. As a result of this structure, a CEO can talk about the roles of each person on the management team so each person, including the CEO, understands what he or she has to do for the upcoming week. Each management team member is held accountable for his or her particular role.

In the marketing industry, businesses offer services, and they sell thoughts and ideas rather than physical, tangible products. Positioning intellectual property, such as how individuals represent the team, is an important component in the marketing business. For example, at Red F, our marketing teams are eclectic in that they come from different backgrounds or from different industries, and are different ages, races, genders, and ethnicities. We generally hire based primarily on intellectual horsepower and an individual's distinctive qualities. This diversity creates different viewpoints and different channels of thought that are huge strategic assets in marketing.

The Importance of Personnel

Once again, the greatest resource for any company is its people. Instead of solving all the problems single-handedly, a CEO should unleash the potential of the team, and facilitate and shape the flow of answers they discover. For example, at Red F, the company conducted an associate survey to determine points that needed improvement. Once these areas were identified through the survey, the company decided to form action teams: one focused on company culture, one focused on training and development, and one focused on business development. As a result, the employees control the actions of and the improvements to the company. We also use a mix of people for brainstorming sessions and strategy sessions with clients.

Frequently at marketing firms, the largest expense is personnel, because the intellectual thought leadership they sell is driven from people. The right people are the critical component of a successful business model. As a result, I tend to hire the right individuals when I find them, and work them into the company even if it's not a perfect short-term fit.

Overcoming Challenges

One challenge of a CEO is knowing when he or she has received enough input to make a well-informed decision, and then just making the call. People often simultaneously want their voices heard and want to be led. As a result, individuals need to know that a CEO is confident in his or her decisions at the time they are made. A team must be confident in the decisions of its CEO, but also must not follow blindly. Similarly, a CEO must be confident in a decision, but must understand that he or she must continually evaluate the effectiveness of decisions as a situation changes.

The second challenge for most CEOs is creating and maintaining an external peer network of individuals that can provide advice and guidance. Through a partnership with external executives, a CEO can create a trusted network of individuals on which to test ideas. I personally have used my network through business organizations like the *Inc.* 500 and Alpha Kappa Psi business fraternity to improve my personal network.

Another challenge of a CEO is managing the constant ups and downs of a business, such as winning a big client and then losing another. Our marketing team and workplace is a constantly changing landscape that morphs when a new person or client is added, or when an old person or client is lost. The best piece of advice I have ever received is that it's never as good or as bad as it seems. A CEO must remain stable and confident, despite the emotional rollercoaster he or she is experiencing.

Successful Strategies

Most importantly, CEOs need a competitive point of difference in terms of positioning a company's products or services. The first rule of positioning is the strategic art of sacrificing items that will, in the end, make a company more relevant to its target audience. For example, Red F does not advertise using mass media such as television, print, or radio, but instead is following the future trend of using more non-traditional elements of the marketplace. This allows us the become experts in this area versus generalists in all areas of marketing. The second thing is showing employees what the end goal is and what it looks like. For example, we describe how our company is working towards changing the future of marketing, rather than just stating that we are trying to reach certain goals. Instead of describing what a company does, a CEO should describe what a company wants to achieve.

Research and Development

One research and development process involves understanding the key growth areas for businesses in terms of thought leadership and intellectual property, and how to track the marketplace trends in those areas. We don't focus on companies as competition as much as who else could provide a solution to our client's problem with their thinking or product.

The second process is creating an idea bank in which great ideas for particular clients or industries are stored. Having this library of thought leadership allows a marketing company to become more productive, maintain intellectual capital after individuals change jobs, and provide better thought leadership to customers. This becomes a physical asset of the thinking of the company, stored digitally for easy reference by employees.

The Changing Role of the CEO

The demand in terms of the pace at which business moves is increasing at an increasing rate. As a result, CEOs must determine the right amount of focus to direct towards particular initiatives that drive the business of a company. There is a cascading effect of focus in any organization. By a CEO remaining 100 percent focused, the focus of lower employees may only decrease to 90 percent, instead of beginning with 80 percent at the CEO level and translating into 40 percent with other employees.

In the future, the fight for talent, the amount of distraction, and the demand for consistent profitability will increase. I think the largest impact in the future will be the necessity to continually iterate and evolve a business model toward greater success. Companies must constantly reinvent themselves before another company does it for them. For example, some CEOs in dying industries refuse to cannibalize their own business with newer products. CEOs constantly need to help their teams struggle to find the next solution and develop the business model to match that solution with a sense of urgency.

In order to adapt to these future challenges, a CEO must remember three words—vision, talent, and environment—in order to simplify the roles of the position and direct a company toward success.

Daniel J. Roselli joined Red F Marketing in 2003. Red F is a strategic consulting and marketing firm blending consulting and marketing execution services focusing on elements of the marketing mix outside of the traditional mass media space. This includes direct marketing, partnerships, Hispanic marketing, brand strategy, and sports and events marketing.

Prior to joining Red F, Mr. Roselli served as senior vice president for Bank of America, vice president for marketing at Allied-Domecq, and marketing director for M&M's candies at Mars, Inc. He also has worked in marketing for Colgate-Palmolive and General Mills.

Mr. Roselli holds a B.A. in financial administration from the Eli Broad School of Business at Michigan State University, and an M.B.A. in marketing from the Carlson School of Management at the University of Minnesota. He is the chairman and founder of the Roselli Foundation for Children.

Leadership in the Health Care Industry

Robert J. Pallari
President and Chief Executive Officer
Legacy Health System

My Role

My primary role is to see that the company is able to achieve both its short- and long-term strategic objectives. I take the development of my management team and the mentoring of my management team very seriously. I have committed to each of them to provide whatever I can that will contribute to their development into CEOs, whether in succeeding me as part of our succession planning or in taking a CEO position with another organization.

I set the benchmarks in terms of pushing us as a management team and as an organization in the areas of productivity, efficiency, quality outcomes, customer services, and in maintaining our social responsibility to the community, which is our mission as a not-for-profit health care system.

In the hospital or health care system business (which is typically multiple hospitals and physician clinics organized and integrated for synergy), the overwhelming percentage of hospitals are not-for-profit. That legal status provides advantages, and also has requirements that publicly traded private businesses do not have. A CEO must balance traditional business objectives with not-for-profit requirements. That not-for-profit mission reflects our values and drives our business decisions.

Our businesses are primarily reimbursed through various forms of tax-supported organizations and government programs, such as:

- Direct government programs like Medicare or Medicaid
- Indirect tax-supported insurance plans that are usually provided to school teachers, municipal works, state workers, federal workers, etc.

Our business is less subject to the broad competitive marketplace forces, but because of the system of reimbursement, we have much less control than most businesses, due to the vagaries of politics and governments.

Finally, most hospitals have not fully employed the physicians in their communities; that means we are staffing a high-tech factory with workers who are in a support role to the main producer of the product (the physician), who is often not an employee. In this type of relationship, there is a loss of control that creates other issues. In some instances, you find yourself ending up in disagreement with your physicians, because the incentives are different. There has traditionally been a degree of friction between hospitals and physicians, even though the casual observer might think they are fully integrated.

In this context, it is critical for a CEO to create a vision others can see, emotionally resonate with, and want to achieve.

Our industry is a people business. It requires the leadership of people and the management of people. Leaders must sincerely enjoy working with people and do better if they have an extroverted personality.

The leaders must also have insatiable intellectual curiosity in regards to everything:

- The business: How can we improve?
- The competition: What are they up to now?
- The market: How solid are the old services? What are the new services? Where's the population growth?
- The customer: What do they need? What do they think of our service?
- The rut: How do I avoid self-satisfaction and continuously seek to improve?
- The mainstream: How do I avoid insular thinking and problem-solving, and force off-the-wall brainstorming to stimulate creative and risk-taking discussion?

Above all the preferred qualities, a CEO must have courage to decide. What distinguishes a successful CEO is not the day-to-day decisions of which most are pretty clear-cut. The great CEO is distinguished by the courage of being able to execute. To make the difficult decisions and take responsibility for them, while also being humble enough to make a mid-course correction if indeed you were wrong. Those are the hallmarks of the successful CEO.

Strategies and Challenges

My first essential strategy is frequent, direct, and honest communication with my stakeholders. Those stakeholders range from my employees to my management team, my affiliated physicians, my board, and my community. I have found over thirty-four years that my successes have more often been a case of providing more and early communication around issues, then of holding back information and trying to recover or solve problems in a state of crisis.

I respect my colleagues' capacity to deal with the unknowns, and I assume they can handle speculation on potential future events. This grants permission to discuss anything and allows us the opportunity to consider the worst case scenarios. This is almost like rehearsing the possibilities, and in rehearsing, a team tends to learn more about how they might react. They anticipate contingencies, and because they feel like they've gone through it before in rehearsal when and if it actually occurs, they are calmer, making better decisions.

The CEO's greatest challenge is trying to find the mutually beneficial ground in working with other people. Generally speaking, our American orientation toward communicating in business is still rooted in competition, where one party wins and the other loses. Our society and culture have not been built upon the art of negotiation, so in any difficult interaction (be it just day-to-day negotiation of what needs to be done or a major contract arrangement), we struggle. We inevitably walk in prepared to do battle, as opposed to seeking a path that will be beneficial for both parties. I always try to think first: "give to get."

One of the CEO's most important resources is a restless mind. Most successful leaders I've had the occasion to meet are people who have restless minds. They do not have the ability to do what most new wave psychology books would tell you to do, which is not to contemplate the future, because you can create anxiety based on a fantasy, because you do not know that future. Almost all successful leaders I know are incredible worriers. They never look in the mirror and believe they are successful. They constantly believe they can achieve more, and always hear footsteps behind them getting closer. Most successful leaders are intrinsically driven and highly competitive, at least within their business world.

Working with Other Executives

Our organization has five senior executives in addition to myself, with whom I work closely. I work closely with our:

- Chief financial officer
- Chief of operations
- Chief medical officer
- Chief legal officer
- Chief administrative officer

Our chief administration officer handles all the behind-the-scenes operational, administrative support services that allow our clinical operation support services to do what they do.

Since I assumed the position of CEO, I've begun to construct the individuals who make up the senior executive team puzzle. I'd rather populate our management team with people who have all the traits necessary for a CEO, because that's going to be good for the growth of the organization, and it's going to be personally good for me: one individual can never achieve the same level of success as a collective group of talented individuals, each of whom perceives his or her job as an extraordinary value and essential to the success of the organization, and each of whom has a clear area of responsibility and accountability. I make sure they do not become siloed, and that they bridge the other parts of the puzzle so we're able to move as a whole and not get out of balance.

When looking for members of this executive team, I look for people with a certain demeanor. I look for a combination of personality types that creates a team chemistry. I'm not looking for five ego-driven, aggressive/combative personalities—we would end up in a civil war. Like any symphony conductor, I'm looking to blend the brass with the woodwinds and the strings; within each of those groups, I'm looking for those who can lead, mentor, and develop the second tier. At this level, I need people who understand the technical and operational aspects of our business, but I'm really looking at those people who have the ability to communicate a vision and execute a plan within their unit that contributes to the overall strategic goals of the organization.

I like leaders who possess a generosity of spirit. Who like to mentor people, delegate responsibility, give credit and not always take it, and develop their own succession. I think the greatest error of a CEO is to look in the mirror and say, "If I could just find five more of the person I'm looking at, boy, things would be terrific." The biggest mistake you can make is to believe you are an icon, that you are indispensable, and that if you could duplicate yourself, you would have the strongest team. That is a recipe for disaster.

Group Goal Setting

We set five-year strategic plans, and in doing so we take a rigorous look back at where we expected to be, and we benchmark ourselves against various metrics to ascertain whether we've achieved those goals. We want to note where in a five-year plan we really misunderstood our projections of the future, and where we made course corrections and adjustments. We then want to understand our current environment. We want to go through a planning process that projects what we believe our environment and market will be over the next five years. We then narrow down two to five major strategic goals we're going to drive toward. We do that together as a broad and deep management team, so at that point I bring in vice presidents and directors. We try to get greater buy-in. We attempt in our assessment to go to the working units, so we get grass-root input and incorporate any ideas that could improve our work product and our work flow. We also involve our affiliated stakeholders. We get input from our physicians, as well as from the community and from our board. It is a formal process, and on a day-to-day basis we keep uppermost in our minds the direction and destination we've set for ourselves.

Our particular industry is not as self-contained and controllable as other businesses. Many people have an interest in our industry and have a stake in our business. We are overseen by some fifty regulatory bodies, so we certainly have to be attendant to and cognizant of the political and regulatory environment. It's a much more complex business today than it ever was, and many believe they are the master of your business. It's better to involve key people early in the process and keep them updated. Having to stop and backtrack to bring people on board is a momentum and morale killer.

Because of this, the number-one piece of advice I give to my team is to take care of your people and stakeholders. Be actively involved with your people and don't distance yourself. There is a tendency, particularly in an information age, to get buried in data, head in the computer poring over spreadsheets. Along the way, you disconnect from your employees, teammates, and stakeholders who are essential for the execution. I insist that my management team stay visible and connected to the people who are the doers.

Leaders must have the courage to make the decisions. When you have enough information, don't delay by thinking you can get more information if you just wait another week, another month. You will get more information, but it probably will not be better or helpful in terms of the decision you have to make. The art is sensing the tipping point between being adequately informed and waiting too long to make a decision, and having the courage to make the right decision at the right time.

I see myself as being a coach of a very diverse and talented team of people. My role is to contribute to the observation of performance, honestly addressing and identifying areas of weakness that need to be improved, and having the courage to call out the elephant in the room—because groups of people inevitably get into uncomfortable confrontations and tend either to snipe or to avoid the issue. I must turn this denial into constructive problem solving, and resolve to move forward.

Back to Basics

One personal strategy of mine is to focus on our fundamental business transactions. The key two or three things I continually monitor that are the essential ingredients to our consistent performance. We have had fifteen years of profitable performance. We're Standard & Poors "AA" rated. Our communities need to rely on us, so stability and consistency of performance and service are our goals. I believe operational efficiency can always be improved. In our industry and mature market, if we can consistently improve costs, then that overtime probably contributes more to our profits than any expectation of added market share.

Secondly, I believe you must excel at your customer service. It is a requisite of doing business, but most businesses fail at it miserably. In a market like mine (where it is very difficult to differentiate yourself from your competitors), you can distinguish yourself in the area of exemplary service. I constantly drive us to be operationally efficient and to provide exemplary service.

Team Expenses and Research and Development

We're a labor-intensive service, so 55 to 60 percent of our cost is in personnel. The next largest area of cost comes in the required supplies we must purchase to be able to deliver the medical service. Then there is the extraordinary expense attached to the technology and capital equipment that is constantly being promoted in our industry. Those are the top three expenses, and it is a consistent challenge to prioritize finite resources and apply some measure of efficacy in order to be able to make good value decisions.

Team research and development efforts are very formalized. We have business development and clinical development staff whose job it is to understand our core businesses and ultimately research emerging technologies. In our business, radical changes are going to be spawned by changing technologies, and we need to commit a formal approach to the assessment of where our business lines or our service lines are technologically and clinically, and where they may be heading. There was a time in open heart surgery when the technical processes used resulted in a twelve-day hospital stay; now, because of technical changes, it's not unusual to have people in the hospital no longer than four or five days. That is a radical change in terms of our staffing, reimbursement, margins, and so forth. If we were asleep at the switch, we could have been budgeting revenue that was never going to take place; we could have found ourselves failing financially, having bet on the status quo and not being cognizant of what the future was going to bring.

Top Challenges

When running a company with thousands of people, as much as we try to hire right and provide challenging family wage-paying jobs, we are going to have our share of mishires, misfits, unhappy people, and destructive people. One of the most important ingredients of a successful organization is to make sure we are trying to prevent this type of employment, but also making sure what we're doing is taking action as swiftly as possible to weed out toxic employees who could jeopardize the health of the overall organization. That takes a top-down commitment and championing; otherwise, there is a general tendency to avoid those confrontations. Most people are intimidated by aggressive people, or by people who are somewhat aberrant in their behavior, so you must give confidence and support to those people. We have to ensure that management is protected and supported, and that you're making a statement to the rest of your employees that you prize their behavior and are not going to waste your precious resources in dealing with the distracters. In that way, you raise the morale of your overall employee workforce.

A second major challenge comes in dealing with doctors. In our business, the incentives for our two businesses are not always mutually aligned. Sometimes, we are in fact pulling and pushing against each other. Our hospital factories would just be empty if we don't have doctors doing their work in our hospitals, so we must maintain the best possible relationships with physicians, but that doesn't mean the only way to maintain those relationships is to meet every need, whim, and request. That just isn't a realistic possibility. Striking this balance takes leadership at the top.

One of the biggest misconceptions about this job is that the CEO has the toughest job. For me, the CEO job is often the most fun job. It is often less intense, particularly if you've done your preparation and have been able to construct a management team and an organizational culture that creates its own momentum and has its own intrinsic drive for excellence. That said, there are those moments that come in your tenure as a CEO that are the reasons you get paid what you get paid—those are truly the test of your capability as a CEO, and that's when the buck clearly stops with you. The decisions have to be made individually, and you test your mettle, your resolve, and your experience. That becomes the exhilarating challenge: do you or don't you have what it takes to be a leader at those few moments when it all comes down to you alone.

Our Changing Role

I think the role of the CEO truly has moved from being the singular head decision-maker to being the ultimate conductor of the symphony or the championship coach. He or she must take individuals with multiple personalities, behaviors, and skills, provide the vision, and then shape, lead, mold, manipulate, and cajole them into a nimble, responsive, mobile management force that can implement the strategic vision.

I'm seeing more and more people in the upper management levels who see themselves as leaders, so there are many fewer individuals who defer and only aspire to the level of a vice president or a senior vice president. Most now aspire to the CEO level. I announced my retirement effective October 1, and four out of five of my senior vice presidents have applied for the job. I see that as an indicator that each in his own mind sees himself as capable of running the organization from within the framework of his own capabilities, experiences, and sense of where the organization should go. This also speaks volumes about the confidence of the executive team based on their experience with the organization.

Amid these changes, the golden rules for being a CEO have not changed. First, never see yourself on the top of organizational chart; see yourself on a continuum of people doing work, all of whom are essential to contributing equally to the success of the organization. Second, don't make the mistake of thinking because of the perks of the job and the personal attention you may receive that you are above others; hubris destroys. Finally, don't get confused—remember the true golden rule: do unto others as you would have them do unto yourself.

Robert J. Pallari is currently the president and chief executive officer of Legacy Health System, which is based in Portland, Oregon. Legacy operates in Oregon and Washington, and consists of six hospitals; seventeen physician clinics, home health and hospice services, and a medical research center; and 8,000 employees. Mr. Pallari has been an executive with Legacy since its founding in 1989. Prior to Legacy, he was the chief executive officer of an HMO, and during the 1970s was a teacher and public health administrator. Mr. Pallari was a primary architect of the Oregon Health Plan, and has served as a health policy advisor to five Oregon governors and three Oregon senators. He serves on a number of boards and is a regular speaker at many health care conferences.

Dedication: *To F. Wm. Pallari, my father, and Peter Pallari, my grandfather, who passed on their wisdom, love, and unconditional support.*

A Focus on Cost Stability

Mark Hamdan

Chief Executive Officer

HRsmart Inc.

Goals and Responsibilities

The central goal of my position is to make sure we keep growing revenue and clients, building new technology applications, and remain profitable while doing so.

My first contribution to this goal is to understand the big picture, the vision, and the strategy of the company, so we can stick to it. I build the team to carry on and implement the strategy, and at the same time to make sure, financially, the company continues to be strong and not overextend itself. Growing revenues and clients implies spending a lot of resources and increasing costs, especially while you're adding new technology and resources. To manage that growth while remaining profitable is the key to my position. My mandate is to grow as fast as possible and add new technology while also keeping cash flow and cost stability in check.

To be successful, a chief executive officer (CEO) needs a clear vision, understanding the future of where the company is going; leadership ability, making sure you hire and lead the right team; and the drive and tenacity to stick it out through the hard times and continue to drive the whole team forward.

Our Unique Focus

One unique aspect of our industry has been our focus on cost stability. In a high-tech growth environment particularly, cost stability is often underplayed. We, however, focus on it, which means we focus on having a low cost structure but, at the same time, also focus on having technological superiority, which is also something companies in our industry typically have not focused on.

One of my personal strategies is to listen to our clients and format our company strategy according to what we hear from them—we do not build our strategy in a vacuum or behind closed doors. Another key strategy is listening to employees internally and adjusting processes, procedures, or focuses to keep them happy and motivated. As in any company, forming a qualified executive team has been key, as is being a coach and a cheerleader for the organization.

Building Relationships with Other Executives

The top executives I deal with regularly are the sales and marketing vice president, the vice president of client services (which, in our company, is akin to a chief operating officer), the chief technology officer, and the chief financial officer. They all need to understand the big picture, and at the same time they need to understand how the pieces work together. I make sure they understand from my end what constraints I have to work within to keep us going on the right track and to keep us profitable as a company, and, most importantly, to keep us growing. I make sure I communicate to them all the challenges I face, so they contribute to minimizing those challenges.

The biggest challenge I face is when the executives start competing among each other. That competition, which is typically normal, sometimes turns unfriendly. That is the biggest challenge I face. I overcome that by communicating with everyone and making sure they understand the value of working together. I guide them on what needs to be done, and coach them. In some cases, that can mean that if there is one person on the team who is causing a lot of the issues, having to ask that person to leave.

When I look for members of my executive team, I look above all for the ability to motivate others and to manage people while keeping cost in mind. It's easy to do anything if you have all the money in the world to do it; the challenge is doing it with limited resources.

I often tell my team members to think like entrepreneurs, to think like you own the company. Whenever you make a decision, think: If this were your company, your money, your decision, what would you do? The second most important piece of advice is to always keep client's needs a top priority.

I ensure that my team doesn't get discouraged when times are hard, and doesn't get too comfortable when times are good. We've had hard times. As a CEO, you sometimes feel you need to simply give up, because there's no other shoulder to lean on—that can get tough, and you can feel like giving up, and that helps me to remember not to do that. At the same time, when we're doing well, sometimes we let down our guard, and that's when things could go wrong. Things aren't going to be good all the time, and if you let down your guard, you could stumble.

I make sure my team members understand the major responsibilities I have: growing the company, adding new technology, and remaining profitable. I make sure they understand that, and that each understands how he or she contributes to that process, and how each one of their actions would lead to success or failure, so they can contribute by doing the right thing.

Personal Strategies

I work hard to identify the market opportunity and understand how it changes. I seek solutions to meet the needs of today, while working on solutions that will be ready, in time, to meet the needs of tomorrow. Every team member is empowered to take part in this exercise and have input into the development process. Another main strategy is hiring a management team that can deliver within the constraints of the business, which in this case are minimum cash availability and profitability constraints. Any manager can do a good job given unlimited resources; those who can deliver with constraints placed around them are true gems. The next strategy is motivating the team, empowering them, and giving them rewards and ownership. It's not about hiring managers or leaders operating in a vacuum; it's about hiring people who are leaders, but who operate as if they were running the whole show, who understand what they do and how it impacts the big picture. Another cultural strategy we employ is creating a counsel of client services, where every decision revolves around making our clients happy.

Research and Development and Team Expenses

In most companies, and especially in our case, adding team members is the most costly activity. Deciding who to add to the team, and when, is a process whose input is sometimes well defined, but more often is not. That is what makes it more of an art and less of a science. For example, hiring decisions in customer service are easy to make, as is adding a salesperson to increase sales revenue. Many others are not as well defined. For example, when do you add software developers? When do you decide to build toward a newer solution? These decisions are effected specifically by input like available cash flow, market changes, competitive environment, and a hundred other factors. Each team evaluates its needs and does a cost-benefit analysis when deciding what to do and when. Typically, I leave that decision to the executive team, but I make sure I communicate with them throughout the process.

Our clients are our research and development department. We work very closely with them to map out their future needs, and try to develop new solutions for the future. Essentially, we let our clients tell us what they need today and what they will need in the future, and we build our solutions around that. The process involves ongoing meetings with clients and prospects, ad hoc informal meetings that take place daily. Formally, we do have a few structured client advisory meetings a few times each year, and we have a client advisory board. Our client services department also meets weekly with our clients, and understands their needs and how they change.

For me, technology is the best resource. I use it to stay informed, to communicate, to plan, and to streamline what I have to do so I can have more time to do what I want to do. The human resources are most important for the company, but for me personally, it's technology.

Most Difficult Situations

Dealing with people issues, feelings, and personal problems are the most difficult situations I face. We try to find the right person in the first place, and in case a person fails, we try to identify every part of every condition, and try to have a "Plan B" in case everything else fails. It's a challenge, because people are not always logical beings. Unlike computers, they do not always react the same way every time you give them the same input, so it's a very challenging process.

The other main challenge is staying the course when times are tough. We had some very difficult times in the company, and we stayed the course, which was very tough. We managed through it, and succeeded. Essentially, if shareholders are happy and results are good, they tend to interfere less with the operations of the company. If things stop going well, then they often intervene; sometimes they're not experienced in the industry or the company, and that may lead to changes in direction that are not optimal. The best way is to keep things running well.

The biggest misconception around my position is that people think the CEO is the boss. I think the CEO is the one that works for everyone else in the company, because the CEO feels his or her role is to make sure everyone in the company is doing a good job, and has the all the resources and support needed to do the job properly. In a sense, the CEO works for everyone else in the company. Granted, employees may feel that CEOs sometimes have to make decisions that may encroach on some people, and that can make them the "boss." However, the only reason they have to make such decisions is that they're trying to protect others in the company, or the company's bottom line, or the team in general. I think of CEOs as the lowest common denominator of support within a company. We essentially support everybody.

Recent and Coming Changes in the CEO Role

CEOs today must have an increased focus on the cleanliness of the internal process, and an increased focus on the ethical disposition of the company. Those two elements, which obviously have been in the news, have been very significant. CEOs are, in a positive way, more inclined to watch very carefully the ethical impact of any decisions the company makes. On the negative side, they're becoming more and more risk-averse, and afraid to make decisions for fear of not meeting certain regulations. I think this trend of CEOs becoming more risk-averse will continue. The actions of a few have made a negative impact on the hundreds of other CEOs who would otherwise have taken calculated risks to improve their companies but who, under the current oversight, hold back and play it safe.

Talent shortages are also going to be a key challenge for any CEO. Smart CEOs will put together a long-term strategy to address those talent shortages, and to build an all-encompassing talent plan that projects the needs of the organization today, and three years into the future. The CEO must also develop programs, not only to find the right talent, but also to develop it as well. If a company knows it will need in three or four years programmers with certain knowledge, the company may be better off sponsoring a program at a certain university to produce this talent, rather than waiting and then trying to find it in the marketplace. These plans should address talent retention as well, which means keeping your current employees or recycling existing talent. Every company has people internally who can be retrained and moved to different positions as they're needed. All of that is in addition to the normal focus on motivating employees, so that we can keep retention high and lose fewer employees.

The Golden Rules

The golden rules for being a successful CEO are:

1. Pick the right team.
2. Communicate, cheer, and coach.
3. Reward success handsomely, and be quick to deal with mediocrity.

The team is the one that's really going to deliver on any strategy. You need to have the right people there, and they need to understand what they are doing, and be excited and motivated to do it. Cheering, coaching, and rewarding them handsomely are key. At the same time, a team is only as strong as its weakest link, so if you as a CEO allow mediocrity to remain, it will bring down the whole team. In addition to rewarding success, dealing with mediocrity will ensure that the team stays in top shape.

Mark Hamdan is an established corporate executive and entrepreneur with a wealth of hands-on experience providing focused leadership, building effective management teams, and creating and then developing profitable infrastructure.

Mr. Hamdan co-founded HRsmart in 1994, formulating the original vision and strategic direction for the company and assembling the current management team.

In other entrepreneurial efforts, he co-founded Directel, a multinational paging company that employed over 500 professionals in Brazil and Argentina. He also co-founded and served as chairman of the board for CNI, an executive recruiting firm, and Careernet, a public career board, both based in Florida.

As a corporate executive, he headed the national indirect distribution for PageNet, at one time the largest paging company in the world. He also held various senior sales and marketing positions for telecommunications conglomerate GTE (currently Verizon).

Mr. Hamdan received his B.E. in computer systems engineering from the American University in Beirut, and an M.B.A. from the University of Texas at Austin.

Dedication: *I dedicate this to my wife, Weeda, who inspires me with her drive and achievements.*

Creating a Financial Impact as CEO

Jane H. Allen
President
Counsel On Call

Introduction

Counsel On Call was started to place well-credentialed attorneys into project positions with law firms and corporate legal departments. Presently, on any given day, we have from one to two hundred attorneys working on a vast array of contract assignments throughout the country.

My ultimate goal is to create an alternative to the traditional practice of law that affords talented attorneys the opportunity to enjoy the challenges of practicing law while still maintaining some balance between their personal and professional life. The company is about providing options to attorneys—an option to the traditional hiring model and an option to the traditional way to practice.

As chief executive officer (CEO) of a high-growth company in an emerging industry, my primary job is to establish the vision for our organization, ensure this vision is understood and shared throughout the ranks, and then lead by example.

Creating Financial Impact

Financial impact for our company can be viewed from two different vantage points: our clients and our candidates.

For our clients, the financial impact is both immediate and direct. In the law firm setting, the use of contract attorneys enables the firm to more closely allocate overhead with workload. When the case settles, the contract attorneys are taken off the assignment and the overhead goes away. This is a stark contrast to the traditional associate-partner model.

For the corporate legal department, the financial impact is also great. Most contract attorneys bill at rates that are one-third to one-half of the billing rates of outside counsel. For most of our corporate clients, the use of contract attorneys on work that cannot justify paying outside counsel rates enables a significant savings.

We create financial impact for our candidates by allowing them to get the highest and best return on their law school education and experience while still balancing professional and personal interests. Most of our candidates would move into a profession less time-consuming and far less lucrative than the practice of law in order to pursue activities outside of work or to have more control over their schedule. Some would even stop working all together. Counsel On Call has allowed these professionals the opportunity to utilize their education and experience, and have the time and control that was missing in private practice.

By far, the largest expense at Counsel On Call is our corporate employees—those that handle sales and recruiting. All are accomplished attorneys in their own right, having performed very well in their chosen profession. We hire people who have both a strong legal background and entrepreneurial skills. In order to get the talent we need, we must offer highly competitive compensation. Therefore, a large part of my role is projecting and anticipating growth, and then hiring the team accordingly.

Being a CEO: The Art

My role as a CEO at Counsel On Call is much different than it would be in a in a large, public company. I like to think of it from a military standpoint—there is the modern day general, leading from behind the scenes, setting strategy, making decisions and putting people into play. Then there is the image of General Custer leading his troops into battle from the front. I'm more like General Custer.

In my opinion, the most critical aspect of my leadership is setting an example. Before entering law school, I was a second grade school teacher. This occupation taught me early on the enormous responsibility of setting an example in everything I did. Ironically, in some ways, I don't view this job much differently. Since I am the most visible person in the organization, my primary role is to set an example for others to follow. I realize that there are eyes upon me at all times, analyzing how I respond to each situation, no matter how small it seems.

In a company like ours, where the CEO interacts with virtually all the employees on a regular basis, a CEO must have visible and uncompromising integrity. It's a given that anyone who is successful has drive and motivation, but employees have to know and respect the core of the person who is leading their company. If they know honesty is always going to come first, that gives them a way to evaluate my performance. I believe integrity and character are essential to success.

A consistent theme I have tried to instill within our organization is to put oneself in another person's shoes in every situation. Just as it is important for all members of my team to respond to one another in a diligent and respectful way, as CEO, I can't react impulsively. I lead by example. I would never ask anyone to do anything I wouldn't do myself.

Unique Aspects of My Industry

There are several aspects of my work as a CEO that are unique to this industry, the primary one being that we are pioneers in a very conservative profession. In specializing in high-level contract attorney placement, we are trying to establish a new career path for lawyers that has not previously existed. As such, there are few, if any direct competitors.

Strategies for Success

In hiring all key people for Counsel On Call—and by key people I mean anyone that has any interaction with clients and candidates—I look for individuals who are passionate about changing the practice of law. With every placement, our people believe we are really creating this "alternative to the traditional practice of law" —one that balances career ambitions with lifestyle choices. I have found that the pride of people who view there job as something much larger than their day-to-day responsibilities can be the single most powerful force in helping the company achieve its goals.

Another great advantage for Counsel On Call is that all of our corporate employees—sales personnel and recruiters—are former practicing attorneys. As a result, we are in front of clients and candidates on a regular basis at bar functions and other industry events. We all experienced while in private practice the need for a company such as Counsel On Call, both from a client's perspective and from a candidate's perspective. Thus, we market as peers. This has proven to be essential in achieving consistent feedback from our market in an environment where we can't conduct research and development from analyzing other companies. Our research and development efforts are based on our communication with lawyers.

Finally, we spend a great amount of time setting measurable goals at Counsel On Call. We have annual goals for each office and quarterly goals for individuals. We measure both objective and subjective goals. We use metrics, because it's important for everyone to understand that the overlying vision is broken down to measurable goals. At the same time, it's equally important for people to understand what they're doing on a daily basis to reach their long-term goals.

Challenges

The two most powerful challenges facing our organization are distractions and evolution.

As a very visible pioneer in a conservative field, I, along with others in our organization, are frequently presented with new opportunities to service the legal profession or innovative ways to provide legal services to consumers. While you never want to stop looking ahead, I have found many of these opportunities can actually impede our growth. Our organization spends considerable time discussing what Jim Collins, in his book *Good to Great*, refers to as the "Hedgehog Concept"—focus on what you really do well and forget about everything else. As a result, we spend almost as much time talking about what we don't want to do as we do discussing our core business.

In a company like ours, growth presents a huge challenge. Evolving from an entrepreneurial one-person shop to a company with multiple offices, multiple layers of management, and a higher degree of job specialization requires constant change on behalf of our employees. While I regularly communicate both the inevitability and the importance of this growth to employees, some people are simply averse to change. Most of our turnover is somehow related to the inability of an individual to grow into a new position.

Finally, while the fact that all of our employees are attorneys is a major advantage on the sales and marketing front, it can occasionally be a challenge on the operational side. Attorneys are trained to identify the obstacles and challenges facing any event. Such focus on the problematic side of a situation frequently leaves too little time for finding solutions. Therefore, another key component of my job is training attorneys to think more like business people.

The Team

I work very closely with the corporate chief operating officer and the heads of each of our offices. Although I have personally performed every job in our organization and am in front on most major sales initiatives and key clients, I don't get highly involved in what happens daily within each office. This works, as long as I have articulated the vision and standards for performance effectively.

In fact, I don't feel like I'm able to be an effective CEO if I'm micromanaging. I tell people to anticipate when something needs my attention. I ask them to take my ideas, talk through the ones they think are worthwhile, put together a package, and bring it back.

In a team member, I look for a person of integrity, character, and good heart. As the company has changed, I need people who can roll with the punches. No matter how well someone performs, if they're not willing to grow and evolve individually as the company evolves, the company will end up growing past them.

I have a five-year goal for the team. We work back from that five-year goal to set our annual goals, and then we work back from our annual goals to set our quarterly goals. We have quarterly meetings with each office's lawyers and an annual meeting with every person in the company. I have daily meetings with the managers from each office. These meetings may only be ten-minute updates, but it is very important for me to touch base on a frequent basis.

The Changing Face of the CEO

In the past two years, I've gone from an entrepreneur who did everything in the company to a person who has had to implement systems, hire a management team, and delegate responsibilities. In the coming years, my role will continue to evolve. I will be less involved in the day-to-day operations of the company, and more involved in talking to managers in different offices to ensure that we're continuing to grow while not losing sight of our vision.

Jane H. Allen is the founder of Counsel On Call. Prior to starting Counsel On Call, Ms. Allen practiced employment law and general civil litigation with the law firm of Trauger, Ney, and Tuke (formerly Doramus, Trauger, and Ney) in Nashville, Tennessee. She also practiced law and managed a regional office for the Kentucky law firm of Sheffer, Hoffman, Thomason, and Morton.

Ms. Allen is a 1991 graduate of the University of Kentucky School of Law, where she served as executive editor of the Kentucky Law Journal. *Upon graduation from law school, she served as clerk to the Honorable Edward H. Johnstone, United States district judge for the Western Division of Kentucky.*

Ms. Allen is licensed to practice law in Tennessee and Kentucky. She is a member of the Tennessee, Kentucky, and Nashville Bar Associations. She is also a member of the Lawyers Association for Women, the Society of Human Resource Management, and she serves on the advisory board of the Middle Tennessee Paralegal Institute.

She has been a featured speaker nationally on various employment law issues, effective hiring and interviewing techniques, trends within the legal profession, the ethics surrounding the use of contract attorneys, and striving to maintain a balanced lifestyle within the practice of law.

Ensuring Growth in the Manufacturing Industry

Jerrold L. Handsaker

President

Innovative Lighting Inc.

United States manufacturing companies need to be global in their vision. They need to be aware of the worldwide competition's abilities so they can devise methods to compete with global manufacturing, not just that which goes on in the U.S. We can be protectionist in some of the things we do, and certainly a domestic manufacturer needs to be aggressive with any offshore manufacturer that is counterfeiting their products to gain a market share without having to go through the efforts the American manufacturer did to create those markets. But more importantly, we must recognize our strengths and take advantage of them.

At Innovative Lighting, we utilize the newest technologies in design, product development, and assembly, much like most other domestic manufacturing companies. Fortunately for us, there are some new technologies that are helping drive our industry right now. Our approach is unique in that, while other companies are seeking to go offshore with a number of their products, we seek to increase our efficiency within our company. We engineer our products to require minimal labor per item from the outset. We work to cut unnecessary components and reduce as many steps as possible in the manufacturing process without affecting the overall quality of the product. By reducing components and the number of assembly steps, we attempt to lower costs to a point that the costs associated with offshore products such as transportation, and large inventory carrying costs, equalize the playing field.

Ensuring Growth

We are a small company. It is easier in a company our size to be hands-on and keep track of revenue trends from the sales and accounting departments than it is in the larger companies with multiple divisions. We have interdepartmental meetings to ensure that all departments are aware of any new customers, products, or projects. To the extent possible, timelines are established and changes are made to ensure that the products are there when they are promised.

We believe our growth has been a product of our willingness to innovate. We aren't satisfied to copy, but rather review a product area without restricting ourselves to what has been done in the past. New technology in the lighting arena has made many new designs possible today that were not a possibility as recently as two years ago. Our mindset together with this new technology has allowed us to grow rapidly, and we believe it will continue to drive our growth for several years into the future.

Challenges

Finding and retaining quality employees is a big challenge for us. We hire talented and independently successful people in many instances, and then it's a challenge to keep them all motivated and headed in the same direction. It can be difficult to prevent them from returning to their complete independence by keeping them challenged as team members rather than independent people. Usually, this can be accomplished by giving a great deal of responsibility to those talented people and letting them manage projects within their departments as quickly as possible. We motivate with economic rewards and with opportunities to gain equity in the company.

Taking Market Share

We try to constantly improve. We listen to our customers' needs and add features to our products so they are more desirable than the products our competition has to offer.

Because of our size, each and every customer we have is important to us. If a customer runs out of a product we were not scheduled to run, we will bump the schedule and handle the customer's need. This simply does not happen with an offshore company, and it gives our customers a sense of security.

Cost and Profit

When we sell a product, we don't have a set margin of how much we expect to make percentage-wise. Some products are new and unique, but have had a large amount of tooling costs or other expenses we have to recover, so we have larger margins on those types of products. We have certain products that have been around long enough to have recovered the tooling costs, and where there is head-to-head competition. The margins in these products are very slim. The product circumstance and the market dictate what the margins are going to be.

Being located in the Midwest has helped keep our overhead and facility expenses low. Component costs had been fluctuating downward due to our increased quantity demands until recent petroleum and metal costs have halted the progress we were making in that regard.

Even so, this mix between new products, unique products, and highly competitive products has allowed us a reasonable degree of profitability for our industry.

Keeping an Edge

The landscape of the manufacturing industry changes rapidly. To keep ahead of these new developments, we have to study industry news reports. Our vendors also help to keep us posted with the latest improvements. We cooperate with them and give them feedback, and so they give us some of the early, pre-release components we design into new products. They give us an early peek at what will be available, so we can start designing with an eye towards what's coming down the line, not what's already there.

We also listen to our customers. We ask them about their needs and what they do or don't like about presently available products. Many times, we can incorporate their needs and eliminate an objection to a product. In so doing, we have developed some very unique products that seem to be getting more and more acceptance within our market.

Measures of Strength

As a chief executive officer of a small company, I enjoy the ability to be actively involved in all of the new product development. I like to attend most department meetings if I'm available. New product meetings regularly take place, and that enables our company to review timelines and know whether or not a product is on target.

There are many ways for measuring success for our company. Remaining profitable so we can stay in business is the obvious one. I like to look at our financial records and make sure we're continually getting stronger financially. We have customers, employees, lenders, and shareholders who are dependent upon our ability to deliver what we have promised. Our employees look for job security and benefits, our customers look for a regular stream of products so they can make their products, our lenders look for loan payments, and our shareholders are expecting dividends. In order to fulfill each of these crucial expectations, we need to be financially strong and see that that financial strength continues to improve each year. As we get stronger, we will be able to offer more and more benefits to our employees, and I think employee satisfaction and loyalty is a measure of our success. We will be able to offer larger dividends to our shareholders, and we believe that is a measure of strength and success. Finally, when all our debts are paid and we can operate debt-free, my wife will believe in the strength of this company.

Industry Changes

The manufacturing industry is growing, and with that growth comes change that is usually driven by needs. Sometimes, the needs can be fulfilled by applying present technology in some new manner. In lighting, maybe we'll find more efficient ballast or use a different source of lighting. Other times, we discover new technology that promises to fill needs, and then we have to find a way of utilizing that new technology. Once we've found a way to use it, we have to get the industry and the customers to embrace it. Many times, this is just a matter of introduction. Most consumers are technology-savvy and are willing to embrace the newest technology if it truly salved a "need." We see companies being more aggressive in accepting and utilizing new technology that becomes available for them in their industries. That technology seems to be, for the most part, generated stateside. If U.S. manufacturers continue to grasp and utilize it, they will remain healthy.

Customer Care

In this industry, being successful means searching for ways to solve customer problems. We have to listen to these customers and create open communication between us and them. They know what they want, and they will give us direction. We need to find ways to serve these needs in a timely and efficient manner with a focus on good customer service.

Getting New Customers

Our vice president of marketing and our sales team are the primary planners for obtaining new customers. We target certain customers or certain segments of the markets in which we operate, and we try to figure out what it is that will attract those customers to us if they're given the right presentation. Then we try to develop that presentation.

Challenges: Customers and Competition

We have to understand the customers' needs. A lot of times, this means being willing to build inventories before we have sales, because the customers are going to be impatient about getting their products. Once they've made their decision, they expect to move on it immediately, and we have to be ready. We always have to make sure the customers are not disappointed with the products or the time it takes to get them.

The sophistication of the competition keeps improving; all companies have to stay on their toes. We have to make sure we have good communications with our customers, so if there are changes in the marketplace, we know about them and can react very quickly. Our competition are very capable, and we do the best we can to be competitive with them. Furthermore, I expect the competition to be increasing. We were one of the early leaders in our particular markets with embracing LED lighting technology. More and more people are entering that market, so I expect to see more and more challenges.

Keeping Customers Interested

There are new opportunities being created for customer acquisition. In our particular industry, the intensity of LED lighting continues to increase. As it increases, we continue to be able to design different products that appeal to different customers. LEDs are light-emitting diodes. They are not an incandescent light bulb, they have a longer lifetime, they don't generate the heat the light bulb generates, they are rugged, and they are much more efficient. With all those strong attributes, it's not too hard to get customers excited about our products.

In order to continue acquiring new customers, we need to prevent our product from getting stale and keep it exciting. Customers can't come back time after time and just see the same product lined up. They have to have a reason to think we're going to stay ahead of the market, or at least equal to where the other competitive manufacturers are. Otherwise, they will feel like they're buying some product that is not as efficient or cutting-edge as the competition's products.

We keep our products interesting by reviewing them on a regular basis. We look at whether there's been any growth or decline in our market, and what our competitors are doing with their competitive products. We stay highly informed as to what new developments are occurring with each of the components that are going into our products. If there have been any improvements, we make sure we don't continue to order the old component when a new component can do the same thing more efficiently or add additional features for the same cost.

Importance of Price

A large portion of manufacturing sales is price-driven, but not all of it. We offer a different technology than what customers are used to, so there's a premium price tag associated with it. If a product is perceived as having additional value and that additional value is recognized not only by our customers, but by their ultimate consumers as well, price won't be the total factor. The main factor is that the product has additional features and attributes.

Customer Relations

Customer service can also become more important than price. How well we back our products is important. Our customers should feel comfortable that we are going to be a partner with them, that if we see they're having some trouble, then it's our trouble as well.

We make sure we have good communications with our customers. We contact them for feedback and don't just communicate with them when we're asking for a sale. We check in to see if there are any problems or new ideas they would like us to develop. We just like to have strong relationships with our customers and listen to their needs.

I think there needs to be someone that not only listens to customers, but also has the authority to get something done for them when they have a need. Customer service people can't just put a problem or request in a basket and expect it to go away. They should be handled as quickly as possible. If the person in customer service can't solve an issue, it goes in front of a committee. We keep moving the issue up the chain until we've reached a resolution for the customer and can give an answer.

At Innovative Lighting, it is important that customers know with whom they are dealing. They should know they have access to whoever's in the chain of command. For the most part, once they have a regular person they call up, they get the same person and not just a voice. By providing that service, we give our customers a comfort level they usually haven't had with some of the large competitors.

After patenting a motorized telescopic stern light for boats (called the PowerLight), Jerry Handsaker founded Innovative Lighting Inc., in 1993 and raised money to develop and market the PowerLight. He has served as company president/chief executive officer and chairman of the board since the company's inception.

Previously, Mr. Handsaker practiced law for twenty-three years with emphasis in business, real estate, tax, and litigation.

Mr. Handsaker is an active member of the National Marine Manufactures Association, the American Boat and Yacht Council, the National Association of Trailer Manufacturers, the Transportation Safety Equipment Institute, and of several technical subcommittees within these organizations.

Not-for-Profit Hospital CEO Lessons

J. Philip A. Hinton, M.D.
Former Chief Executive Officer
Community Medical Centers

A CEO in the Health Care Industry

The goals of a chief executive officer (CEO) in the not-for-profit health care profession are to accomplish the missions established by the board of trustees. For most hospitals, the missions may be stated simply: improve the health of the community and promote medical education. Taking good care of patients is the number-one priority. For everyone in the company to understand and participate actively, they must have a picture in their minds about what this really means. An easy way to state this is called the "my mom" standard. That means each hospital employee would take care of patients the same way they would take care of loved family members. That particular goal is really easy to understand. It means an employee would take great care for the patient's safety, convenience, comfort, and well-being. There are certain safety criteria and courtesy criteria that anyone would want achieved if someone were to take care of their mother. So the first goal of a health care CEO is making sure the customers (the patients) get safe, effective care. And the second goal of a CEO, which is just as critical, is maintaining financial stability.

Community Culture

Employees must be focused on the importance of the company's culture, the "my mom" standard. That applies to friendliness with other customers as well, especially with doctors. The hospital industry has a major difference from manufacturing and other service industries in that one of the primary customer groups is doctors who use the hospital as a workshop. In most instances, doctors are not hospital employees. They work in the hospital, but they don't work for the hospital. They are paid independently by the patient or the insurance company. And in most cases, the doctors work in more than one hospital, including hospitals competing with yours. Patients do not usually choose the hospital. They go where their doctor recommends. This means doctors are the primary source of patients for the hospital. And this means the economic viability of the hospital is dependent on its good relationships with the doctors. So treating doctors with respect is really important.

A CEO should always be looking for new markets and new possibilities opening up in the community and surrounding areas in order to make financial improvement to the company. In addition, fundraising can be beneficial, especially when not-for-profit companies or public hospitals have a lot of indigent people who are using services and not bringing money into the company. This makes it important that a CEO be able to go out into the community and ask for gifts. The members of the community get the benefit of seeing their contributions do something worthwhile, and the not-for-profit hospital gets the benefit of the dollars to help the less fortunate.

A Science and an Art

A CEO must set a good example. People watch what the leader does even more than they listen to what that leader says. So the "my mom" standard depends first on how the CEO applies it in everyday actions. Everyone is watching. And if the CEO does it, everyone will follow suit. A CEO must be a good listener. Listening is a skill. The CEO must listen to leaders in the community, to direct reports, to the board of directors, and to everyone else. There is a tendency in executive officers to think they have heard it all, know it all, have seen everything, and to criticize ideas as they come in. A CEO needs to learn that instead of criticizing people and ideas, he or she has to look for the value in what the other person is saying, and encourage that person to pursue that part of their idea to see if it really has value for the company. And don't forget that the quality of the finished project is what's important, not who receives the credit for creating the product.

There is a tendency for CEOs, or for any managers, to want to be liked. It is important for a CEO to make that a secondary consideration, and instead focus on getting things done and negotiating agreements, to be respected instead of liked. There are going to be times when a manager has to say no, and there are times when the directness of that answer will anger people. It is important to be clear and accurate, to say things plainly, instead of just trying to please people.

A CEO needs to create simple ideas people can understand and adopt. A CEO must have a clear vision of where he or she wants the company to go, what he or she wants the company to be. That vision has to be so clear that everyone can see it, and believe it can be accomplished. It cannot be a "vision statement" created by a management group retreat, laminated, put on the wall, and expected to permeate into the company. The vision has to be expressed in a way that explains why the CEO loves the company, its future, the employees' place in those plans, and how the company can ultimately make a difference in the world. That vision must be explained constantly and pushed all the time so people adopt it for themselves.

A strategy or methodology that is absolutely important to a CEO is the ability to focus on one thing at a time. There's a tendency for people to think they can multitask, but action or accomplishment really comes one thing at a time. Of all the things that need to be done, the CEO must figure out what needs to be accomplished first, figure out how to get there, get an agreement with people on who will do what and by when, and then follow through until that one thing is accomplished. This is the only road to progress. The rest is just running in place.

Overcoming Challenges

The CEO must be optimistic. A person can look at a challenge and become discouraged, or that person can look at a challenge and see an opportunity. The CEO must be able to see the opportunity inherent in any challenge. A CEO in a not-for-profit organization often has an unpaid volunteer board of directors that usually includes people with business experience and people without business experience. Some of the people will have a community viewpoint and want the company to do work on projects that are good for the community but do not make money, while others may feel that if a project will not make money, then it should not be done. It is impossible to please everyone. The best way to manage that type of situation is to present the competing viewpoints, show how best to balance them, offer a recommendation, and then let the opposed groups fight about it until they reach agreement. An executive officer is supposed to execute the will of the board of directors, not impose his or her will on them.

Another challenging aspect of being a CEO is the tendency to want to do things alone. There is an inclination to take over projects and just get them done when subordinates don't complete projects or when subordinates do them incorrectly. The answer is to make clear agreements with each direct report, about who does what, and by when. It's really important to accept that subordinates are going to make mistakes. A particularly difficult challenge is dealing with subordinates who aren't performing, who can't or won't live up to their agreements. Instead of taking the project from them, it is best to help them focus, build them up, talk about the agreement they made to complete the project, and get a result. It's important to let them carry the project through to the point where they either accomplish it or they accomplish proving that they can't. If they cannot complete projects, then they need to be replaced.

The Unique Hospital Industry

The majority of hospitals in this country are not-for-profit. In 1945, laws were changed so communities could own hospitals through not-for-profit corporations. This means the shareholders are the people in the community. This puts the hospitals in the public eye. The whole ideology of a not-for-profit hospital is that the hospital is responsible to the public and to the local community to improve their health. One of the most unique aspects of this country's hospital industry is that hospitals are mandated by law to provide hospital care to everyone in need, but this is a mandate with no funding. Federal law requires that a not-for-profit hospital must take anyone who shows up in the emergency room, regardless of their ability to pay. If a person presents to the their hospital emergency room with a problem they believe to be an emergency, the hospital is required to treat that patient until that condition is stable, without even asking whether the patient has the funds or the insurance to pay for it. That legal requirement does not come with any federal funding. To apply the same concept to grocery stores, it would mean they would have to provide food to anyone in need, whether they could pay for it or not. And the grocery store would have to wait until the customer was checked out, to find out if they would be paid or not. And if the customer couldn't pay, they get the food anyway.

In addition to this federal emergency care requirement, in California, hospitals have a nursing ratio requirement. They must have one nurse for every five patients on a general medical ward. This ratio is mandated by state law, without funding to pay for the extra nurses. Underfunded government payment programs are another challenge. Medicare and Medicaid are the main government payment programs. One is for the aged and one is for the poor, and there are many federal requirements that go with these programs. The cost of caring for many Medicare and Medicaid patients exceeds the payments from these government-sponsored programs. It is incredibly challenging to find supplementary sources of payments and donations to make up for what's mandated by law, but not paid for.

Many not-for-profit hospitals are going to have problems in terms of lack of funding. In general, Medicare doesn't pay for itself, and Medicaid doesn't pay for itself, and the job of the executive team is to find a way to balance the books. This usually means finding ways to increase the volume of insured patients that do cover their costs to add funding to cover the government programs that don't. The job of the executive team is to find some way to make the company financially viable and still meet the needs of the patients.

The Executive Team

A CEO works most closely with the chief financial officer (CFO), the chief medical officer, and the chief operating officer. To a lesser extent, he or she may work closely with the chief information officer. The best way to work with the executive team is to listen to them. For example, there's a tendency to think the CFO is the person who is responsible for all the finances of the company. That's really only true to the extent that they're responsible for reporting them accurately. They're responsible for giving advice on what areas might be built up and what areas might be taken back a bit to achieve better finances, but they're not the person who actually does it. They're the reporter, and their job is to make sure the CEO and everybody in the company knows exactly how the company is performing. It's really the operations officer that is in charge of productivity and making the changes that are necessary to get the performance the CFO is recommending.

What a CEO really needs to do is listen to the executive team carefully, understand the value in what they're saying, and then get them together in a room to get agreement on what action needs to be taken. Essentially, it does not matter how a company sets up its organization chart. The only thing that counts is having good people as leaders in the company. A company needs to hire people who get things done, who have a bias to action, who listen, and who don't have big egos. Once a company has good people, it doesn't make any difference how they are arranged, because the company will get results.

Team Skills and Goals

The team needs to accomplish set goals. The team should have a bias toward action. A team player is a person who creates things. People who can focus, who can say this is what I want to accomplish, who can plan how to get there, and who actually act and get things done, and create something, are excellent members of a team. Some people already behave that way, but most people have to learn that behavior. If the CEO sets goals, does things to make progress toward them, and takes chances, then the team will learn to do the same by his or her example. Any time a goal is set and a person has to take chances, there is an opportunity to make mistakes. A CEO has to learn to reward that kind of risk-taking behavior. Progress toward a goal entails some risk.

Team Meetings

The way to set goals is to meet as a team. Depending on the size of the project, it might be best to meet as a small team. Goals are agreements, and the agreement is who is going to do what and by when. What a team is really doing in a meeting is negotiating an agreement. A CEO should watch what people are saying and watch for body language in others that indicates they don't agree. If somebody doesn't openly disagree, but their body language shows disagreement, the CEO should call them out and ask them what they are thinking. The CEO should get all the opinions out in the open. Then once a goal is agreed upon, the details—such as how important is it, what kind of priority does it have, and who is going to take it on—get assigned to a person who then starts working with their team. Team members need to stay focused. It is really, really easy to get scattered. There are always twenty more things to do and no time to get them done. The job of an executive is not to get it all done. The job of an executive is to get the things they decide are the most important done.

Doctors and Patients as Friends

A recommendation, especially relevant to the medical field, is to learn to see doctors and patients as friends. Doctors and patients are customers. The business they bring into a hospital pays for employee vacations, employee salaries, and pays for employees to put their kids through college. Employees need to see doctors and patients not as enemies, problems, and competitors, even though they sometimes are all three of those things. Hospital employees need to see the immense value doctors bring to the company, and treat them accordingly.

Specific Strategies

There are two strategies a CEO in the hospital industry can execute to help a company grow and achieve more profits. The primary strategy is to attract and retain superior doctors. Specifically, that means attracting doctors who have good results, good efficiency, and good profitability. The secondary strategy is to differentiate from other hospitals by providing these particular physicians special service and equipment in order to increase their productivity and earn their loyalty. By concentrating on superior doctors, a hospital can become recognized as a center of excellence with demonstrable superior outcomes.

People are Expensive

The biggest expense for any company is in human resources. In hospitals, nearly 50 percent of all expenses are for people. The largest group is nurses. And because there is significant risk in modern health care, the hospital industry is incredibly focused on hiring good people. In recent years, the nurse ratio mandates have made this even harder. In California, in the past, one nurse was able to take care of ten patients, the number then decreased to six, and now a nurse may only take care of five patients at a time on a medical ward. Thus, a hospital must hire more nurses, but the mandate did not offer funding for the increase, and there is a significant nurse shortage nationwide.

Research and Development

Any person on the executive team should be able to come up with new ideas for research and development. Once the idea is discussed, it should be assigned by negotiation and mutual agreement to a specific person to head a work group to evaluate that particular opportunity. Then the executive team will track the progress. The idea will require an initial feasibility report that does not need to be detailed, because the team will need to decide whether to further research or discard the idea fairly quickly so they do not spend money on non-viable ideas. If the idea looks viable, the person in charge of the project will write a full business plan.

A Difficult Situation

The most difficult situation a CEO can face is the inadequate performance of an executive. The first step in handling the situation is to get agreement with the person as to what it is they're supposed to accomplish. Get them focused on their job by outlining specific accomplishments in specific areas. The tendency of a CEO is to simply inform an executive of their job function, and that is not helpful to the executive. A CEO must listen to them talk about what they can't do, get their agreement on what they can do, and then focus on one or two things they have to accomplish, and then help them do it. A CEO should ask what resources and help they need, and then get them that help. If the executive is not performing to the agreement, then they will not last in the company.

The hardest situation anybody in management handles is how to get people to perform at their highest levels. It is impossible to manage people, but it is possible to manage agreements. If a person agrees to a goal, then they are likely to accomplish it. If they simply promise to attain that goal, then they are more likely to fail. An executive who fails repeatedly can no longer be a part of a company.

The primary resources of any company are the people it employs. Selecting good people is a skill every CEO needs to develop. It is really important to interview people and use layering questions to understand the real reason they left their last job, how they feel about people, and so forth. A CEO has to learn to really listen to people, ask appropriate questions, and focus on one thing at time.

The Misunderstood CEO

The biggest misconception about the role of CEO is that the CEO is the absolute boss and can do what he or she wants. That is a complete misperception of what a CEO is and does. A CEO executes the will of the board of directors. He or she executes the will of the company owners. Leadership is really about example. It's about building people up and helping them exploit new ideas. It's about making goals clear and focusing on results, and letting other people get the credit.

The Changing Face of the CEO

In the future, a CEO is going to need management skills. For example, the CEO is not going to just tell people what to do, but is going to help people focus on a few things and listen for the value in what people have to say. The CEO is going to have to make sure the company finances are transparent to everybody, including the workers and the shareholders. Outside fundraising is going to become even more important. Outside fundraising can either mean asking people for money or working out how a company can get supplemental funding from the government.

The Golden Rules

There are three golden rules to being a successful CEO. The first one is to be a good example. The CEO must model the behavior they expect to see in the executive team. The second rule is to share with the executive team the reasons to love the company, how the company makes a difference, and the future of the company. The third rule is to focus on one thing at a time, get agreement on how to get it done, and manage that agreement.

J. Philip A. Hinton, M.D. was president and chief executive officer of Community Medical Centers in Fresno, California, from 1996 to 2005. Prior to that time, he served as medical director for quality management for the hospital system, and was medical director of the California Vascular Institute. As chief executive officer, he grew

Community from a two-hospital, 550-bed system to a four-hospital, 890-bed system with $680 million annual revenue and 6,200 employees. He integrated the Fresno County hospital, a 274-bed public safety net hospital into Community's private system in 1996. Dr. Hinton built a joint venture sixty-bed specialty heart hospital, with physician investors holding 49 percent and CMC holding 51 percent. He also built a new $150 million trauma/critical care building for the Community Regional Medical Center. Two of his four hospitals achieved the PEP-C III top "Three Star" rating for patient satisfaction in 2004. In addition, he developed Community's weekly half-hour television health program, "MedWatch," airing on Fresno's NBC affiliate, KSEE 24.

Bring Your Common Sense and Sense of Humor, but Leave Your Ego at the Door

Neil W. Matheson

Chief Executive Officer

AXIS Healthcare Communications LLC

My Goals as a CEO

The main goal of my position as chief executive officer (CEO) is to create an environment in which every employee can contribute to the best of their ability to the success of the enterprise. I want people to be able to use their present skills and develop new skills in order to grow the business.

A business grows in many different ways—growth of sales, growth of revenues, and growth of profits. One of the most important—and often overlooked—forms of growth is that of the maturity and skill sets of the people in the organization.

Creating Financial Impact

There are several things I do to create direct financial impact and add value to the company. The first is building client relationships. The second is ensuring that the company is funded and financed appropriately. The third is creating a productive work environment.

Every business needs strong client relationships in order to succeed. We're in the service business, so customer satisfaction is one of the most essential elements of our business. If we don't make sales, we go out of business. We're in a business that has a lot of opportunities for growth. These growth opportunities have to be funded. Making sure the company is financed properly is important for growth. The only way the company can grow is if people feel they are respected and that their contributions are valued. Employees have to consider the workplace a fun environment and want to come to work when they get up each morning.

There are several strategies I've developed to help the company grow and achieve more profits. The first is to provide multiple services under one umbrella. The reason we have eight different companies in the group is that each of those companies is a specialty service provider. They can provide services on their own or in conjunction with one another. Our strategy is to be able to provide an individual client with as many different services as possible from under the one roof.

The practice of offering multiple services has really helped us grow. We're bringing in additional revenues from different customer segments while spreading the risk of losing business in any one segment. If one part of the business suffers from negative market force factors, then another part of the business can pick up the slack.

The other strategy I developed for this business is not necessarily unique, but very few companies do it. We link a dedicated medical director who understands the science and medicine around a product with a client service person who is knowledgeable about strategic marketing. The combination of science and strategy creates a unique knowledge base that many of our competitors haven't been able to establish. A lot of agencies use freelance support to develop their content. Our strategy is to have those resources on staff as part of our team so we become a value-added resource to our clients. Creating solid, long-term client relationships has greatly improved the profitability of the business.

The biggest expenses my team incurs are people costs and salaries. The cost of employment is high. When we have additional money to spend, we decide as a team where our priorities lie. Because our greatest expense is people, we have a fairly rigorous method for approving new hires—it's costly to make a mistake.

Our profits are directly related to the amount of revenue we produce, minus our people costs and our overhead. We're essentially selling brainpower. Our whole business is centered on decisions about spending money on more people, so it's an integral part of the way our team functions on a daily basis.

What it Means to be a CEO

Being a CEO means being a facilitator and a coach. As a facilitator, a CEO makes key decisions and helps create the platform on which everyone else performs. Coaching people to use their own skills in order to grow and experience new things also directly impacts the results of the company.

In order to be successful, a CEO needs to be incredibly comfortable with his or her own skill set. He or she has to be charismatic, confident, and able to allow others to excel. He or she needs to allow his or her employees to contribute and grow without his or her own ego getting in the way.

There are three golden rules to being a CEO. The first one is to set a challenging standard that is still attainable by everyone. Next, you have to be willing to hire people who are better than you and provide them with the foundation to excel. You can't be afraid to give these people as much opportunity to succeed as possible. Finally, you have to remember to leave your ego at the door.

The ability to succeed in the CEO role is directly related to self-imposed barriers to success. Those barriers more often than not relate to your own understanding of who you are as an individual. For example, if you set high standards of performance and demand ethical behavior in your business, you can't go out and cheat during a round of golf. There is a very interesting statistic that 75 percent of CEOs play for money on the golf course, and 70 percent have cheated at least once.

You can't set standards for the company and not set an example in your personal life. There's no room for double standards in the CEO role. Inherent in this is the ego factor. People cheat at golf because of their egos. They are embarrassed about the prospect of losing to someone who is better than they are. If they can get over their egos, overcome the desire to compete with their best people, and focus on their role in the organization as a leader, motivator, coach, and mentor, they will more readily succeed.

Unique Aspects of My Industry

To succeed in this business, you really have to understand the biopharmaceutical industry, which is very unique. We are providing a service that is not seen by the public, and therefore not readily understood. We work with highly scientific subject matter that is often so new and cutting-edge that some of the best brains in medicine don't yet fully understand it. We work on very large projects that are often valued at several hundred thousand dollars, and we are essentially selling people's brain power. You therefore can't hire a CEO from another type of business and expect them to be successful in this industry. You need several years of experience under your belt in order to know how this type of business can operate profitably.

Our business is a lot more entrepreneurial than most companies. The marketplace is constantly evolving, and I need to be incredibly flexible in the sense that I have to adapt and innovate on the fly and rely on my years of experience in the industry when making important decisions about the business. Even with that, I learn something new every day.

Strategies for Success

One of the theories I've always subscribed to is the power of teamwork. No matter what someone's skill level, if they work well with others, they'll always do better than they would on their own. I like to get people in an environment where they understand what it means to be part of a team. This includes how to participate as a team member and how to respect others on the team.

A lot of companies talk about teamwork, but when you actually ask their employees to define it, they don't understand what it means. They don't understand that they have to contribute and work as part of a team before it can become a team. It is more of a label to them than an actual cultural, behavioral phenomenon.

In our business, we have various daily online news services that alert us to hot topics. These topics include anything related to the pharmaceutical industry, medicine in general, and critical breakthroughs in new science. We live on that type of information. It allows us to evaluate opportunities for new business and keep up with where science is heading.

I don't feel the need to read a lot of magazines about business. I read books that provide interesting and stimulating ideas. I don't need to constantly look at other forms of information, like CEO support services. At the end of the day, my job is common sense. It's important to understand the business and what's going on in that marketplace, but beyond that I believe the greatest asset you can have is sound judgment and good old common sense.

We don't do a lot of formal research and development for new ideas that impact the company. We come up with ideas and then evaluate opportunities by talking to clients, but we don't do a lot of formal market analysis. Our business is just not conducive to that type of evaluation.

Challenges

One of the most challenging aspects of being a CEO is allowing the business to be directed and managed by others. As the company grows, you have to allow people to take responsibility and lead different parts of the development. You can't continue to be the person who makes all of the decisions.

One real challenge is moving from being the person who starts, initiates, and grows the business to the person who allows others to do that while you lead. It's tough to determine when you should be involved and when you shouldn't be involved in the process of letting the business manage itself. It's been a real challenge for me, because I'm very much a lead-by-example sort of person, but I can't lead by example in every part of the business every day. It's not possible to be in ten different places at once.

The most difficult situations I'm faced with in this position are usually people-related. Differences in personality and conflicts between team members need immediate resolution. Situations where clients are abrasive also need my guidance. This must be done very sensitively, given the fact that we rely on clients for our business. We can't have employees feeling threatened or intimidated by clients, and that can be a real issue in the service business. I've always encouraged people within the organization to hire people who are patient, tolerant, and flexible when it comes to interpersonal skills. Those people rarely experience the type of situations that could potentially arise.

The biggest misconception about my role is that a CEO has to be in an ivory tower or a corner office where no one ever sees him or her. Some people think this is a secretive job, and that I'm surrounded by security and inaccessible. That's not the way I want to conduct business.

I actually walk around with a cup of coffee every morning and talk to people about their weekend, their kids, and their interests and hobbies. I have an open door policy, and I don't like closed door meetings—it breeds mistrust. People call me Neil, not Mr. Matheson. By showing them that I'm simply another person with a role to play, and that I do things with my family on the weekend just like they do, I become more accessible. I have an interest in other people. At the end of the day, my CEO title doesn't change the fact that I'm just as accountable as everyone else in the organization.

The Team

As CEO, I work very closely with the chief financial officer, chief talent officer, and the chief operating officer, as well as the presidents of each of our operating companies. We have eight different operating companies, and a separate president runs each one. My job is to help these presidents understand the way in which the financial performance and the people performance of the business directly impact our success. We set standards for the quality of performance in those areas and make sure processes stay in line with our cultural and philosophical base.

I want to treat everyone within the organization fairly, and we can only do that if the human resources department subscribes to the principles and philosophies we set. It comes down to being a close-knit team. I have to encourage people to implement programs with respect to the culture and philosophy of the company. One of the ways I have done this is to call our human resources department the "valuable resources" department instead of "human resources." It's another way of walking the walk and not just talking the talk.

In my team members, I look for interpersonal skills and the ability to tolerate and understand different issues within the organization from a people management point of view. If there are any disruptive personalities on a team, it's much harder to get everything going in the same direction. Having said that, I don't discourage constructive debate—it's very healthy to respect each others differing point of view.

Our operating board consists of the chief financial officer, the chief technology officer, the chief operating officer, the presidents of the companies, and me. We set our own goals for the growth and development of the business, and for overall performance. We monitor progress every quarter against those goals. The benefit of this is that each board member has a small ownership interest in the business. The reward of meeting our goals is directly reflected in the board members' ability to increase the value of their shareholding.

I often tell my team members not to be reactive, because there are many sides to a story in business and in life. There are always countless reasons why something is the way it is, and until you understand those reasons, overreacting will make the problem worse than it already is. With highly motivated people, there is a tendency to tackle a problem head on and get it solved immediately, but patience is a very important aspect of business. Listening carefully to every point of view will allow you to create the right solution.

The best piece of advice I ever received from another CEO is to do more listening than talking. People who find themselves in leadership positions are very motivated and confident in making decisions. They want to stamp their authority on a situation.

Leadership is about not being the authoritative figure, but rather being the quietly confident and charismatic leader who allows others to talk and make decisions. Afterward, you can put your seal of approval on those decisions and direct them in a way that makes people feel like it was their decision. This way, it looks like you agreed with their stance and approved the decision rather than being a dictatorial leader.

Changing Roles

In the past few years, there has been a big move away from the military model and hierarchal structure of businesses past. This model had an approach of "yes sir," "no sir" and encouraged performance by fear or failure. Part of the move away from this is due to the huge impact of the Internet, the MTV age, and the X-Box generation. In modern business, companies have to lower formality in terms of people relationships to allow people to be productive.

Businesses have to be flexible, adaptive, and innovative. The gap between a new recruit who just graduated from college and a CEO who is forty-eight years of age is not a huge one, but it has to be bridged nonetheless. Companies must understand the dynamics of the world new graduates are coming from in order to integrate them seamlessly.

When I was in college, I submitted all of my projects on paper. I was lucky if I had a typewriter. College students are now submitting projects electronically in PDF files. It's a completely different world. We've got bright young people joining the company who don't subscribe to the same rules of relationships that my parents did. The formality of relationships has changed, and the hierarchies have been broken down. There's been a massive change in the way companies look at the dynamics of the workplace. Harnessing talent and directing productive effort requires a completely different set of skills in today's world.

The basic responsibilities of the CEO will always be the same. The CEO provides a vision, a reason to believe, and the motivation to strive for success. Everybody looks for leadership. It doesn't have to be an attitude of following the leader into the valley of death. It can be more empowering and equal.

Neil Matheson joined the pharmaceutical industry in 1983 as a sales representative for Ciba Geigy New Zealand Ltd. During his time with Ciba Geigy, Mr. Matheson was involved in the launch of Voltaren, the world's largest-selling NSAID.

From 1984 to 1987, Mr. Matheson was a sales and marketing director with New Zealand's largest importer of medical and hospital products. In this role, Mr. Matheson was responsible for negotiating major supply contracts with the New Zealand Hospital Board, as well as representing various specialty surgical products.

In 1987, Mr. Matheson joined Adis International, a global medical publisher, to manage its New Zealand operations. He was responsible for advertising sales for four medical journals and two drug directories, as well as the sale of custom publications to

New Zealand pharmaceutical companies. Mr. Matheson also filled the role of regional manager to South East Asia for a twelve-month period prior to being transferred to the United States to help develop the medical communications division of Adis North America, Inc. He was named executive vice president, North America, in 1990, and participated in a management buy-out in 1991.

In 1999 Mr. Matheson co-founded ApotheCom Associates LLC, a full-service medical communications company providing advocacy development, publication planning, and medical education services to the pharmaceutical, biotechnology, and medical device industries. When Mr. Matheson started Helix Medical Communications LLC in 2000, he also founded AXIS Healthcare Communications to be the holding company and owner of the two agencies. The vision is to provide services to pharmaceutical, biotech, and device companies through the entire product lifecycle.

Mr. Matheson serves several charitable organizations as a member of the board of trustees. He is an active member of the Healthcare Marketing Communications Council and is chairman of HMC University (an educational initiative of the Healthcare Marketing Communications Council). He also is a frequent speaker at industry conferences on medical communications, physician education, and pharmaceutical marketing.

Mr. Matheson has a degree in exercise physiology from the University of Otago, Dunedin, New Zealand.

Leadership: Practical Suggestions for Dedicated Wannabes

Kevin Grauman

Founder, President, and Chief Executive Officer

Outsource Group

Leadership: Top Ten Attributes for Greatness

If you were to perform a Google search for the phrase "executive leadership," approximately 490,000 outcomes will appear in less than one second. In browsing these outcomes, what becomes convincing is that there appear to be more associated concepts, discussions, and attributes on leadership than one can hope to easily digest. It looks to be wholly overwhelming.

Clearly, much has been written on the topic, and much will be contributed to the debate in the future. However, the author respectfully submits that the one universal "truth" is the fact that leadership, executive or other, involves difficult-to-train and intangible personality attributes and styles, rather than tactical and job-specific performance criteria.

Tom Peters, considered by many to be a modern day business management guru, paraphrased it best: "Management is about arranging and telling. Leadership is about nurturing and enhancing." In a similar vein, Dwight D. Eisenhower contended that, "Leadership is the art of getting someone else to do something you want done because he [or she] *wants* to do it."

Interestingly, too, executive leadership, in its own right and by definition, is not the panacea. Rather, it must be relevant, meaningful, and impactful both to the organization as a whole and to the individuals who support it and are impacted by it.

And, while we could continue to debate and postulate yet another version of the apparent "truth," this author's various research has produced a listing of the top ten attributes that present a fairly comprehensive set of leadership characteristics, qualities, and attributes.

1. **Visionary** – It is both necessary and critical that leaders have the ability to define, communicate, and inspire a practical, relevant, and clear vision. This vision should be updated and adapted as circumstances change. Leaders must be able to think about the future and how they will propel, guide, and adapt their businesses in the face of uncertainty and unfamiliarity; otherwise, the past will continue to be both the present and the future, and the organization will likely experience atrophy. By not

"stretching" a company's resources, offerings, and capabilities, a company will not see long-term rewards. Businesses thrive on a sense of purpose and direction, and leaders have a continuing obligation to be fanatical about a larger-than-life vision.

2. **Communicative** – Succinct, consistent, and optimistic communication to all levels within a company, regardless of the nature of the messages, is a fundamental attribute of all good leadership. Vital, too, is the encouragement of constructive feedback and disagreement, to tell it like it is, say what you mean, and keep it simple. Active listening, rather than merely hearing and being readily available and accessible, is essential if communication is to be effective and embraced as a reality.

3. **Deliver on the promise** – Nothing erodes confidence faster than a series of broken promises. And, since we participate in a world based on action, the ability to consistently "walk the talk" and deliver upon prior commitments often constructs a solid leadership backdrop.

4. **Responsible** – There is, generally, wariness for finger-pointing and assignment of blame. Effective leaders take responsibility for decisions that they have made or participated in, regardless of whether their outcomes are successful.

5. **Humble** – Followers disdain arrogance and brashness, since they are often associated with self-serving egotism in a leader. In contrast, too, conventional wisdom reveres modesty, humility, and reserve.

6. **Trustworthy** – Trusted leaders select employees because they are intelligent, perceptive, and empowered. In turn, followers often follow without having to know the entire story or picture. Their buy-in is for their perceived long-term gains, rather than short-term ones. Employees tend to inspire others to share their burden, and those of the business they are supporting in tough times. They, too, understand the need to withhold sensitive information at certain times, and the need to present a united front at other times. Eroded trust usually labels itself as dishonesty and deceit, which are difficult, likely impossible, to amend easily.

7. **Capable** – Leaders continually demonstrate competence, impressive aptitude, mercurial thinking, resourcefulness, and limitless capacity for almost anything they feel passionate about. They delegate with conviction and are passionate about teaching and mentoring, not training, their followers. And, in each successful mentoring relationship there is an expectation for mutual learning—the apprentice from the leader and the leader from the apprentice. Most importantly, common mentoring methodology is one that assists in problem solving by coaching independence of thought rather than becoming a solution provider. A direct product of this approach is that positive character traits in followers are nurtured, thereby assisting both their professional development and their well-being. Leaders learn how to effectively take risks on people, not on circumstances, through empowerment.

8. **Decisive** – Making timely decisions, which are intelligent and unwavering, means that, in some instances, the outcome is failure. This is acceptable, almost expected, by followers. Making an effective decision is more important than the outcome itself. Effective leaders, by virtue of having made these leaps (successfully or not), become better skilled at ensuring successful outcomes, thereby instilling ongoing confidence.

9. **Authentic** – Principled by both high ethics and unbridled integrity, leaders regularly demonstrate a high correlation between their core behaviors, beliefs, and principles and those they expect to be present in their followers. Consequently, leadership embodies the persona of the leader that manifests regularly, consistently, and unwaveringly without the need for hidden agendas or questionable intent.

10. **Genuine and respectful** – Leaders naturally garnish respect primarily for who they are, rather than for what they know. They are even-handed in their dealings with others and can relate to or validate others regardless of domain, tenure, seniority, or context.

Lao-Tzu (the father of Taoism) summed it up best: "The wicked leader is he who the people despise. The good leader is he who the people revere. The *great* leader is he who the people say, 'We did it ourselves.'"

The Personality of Leadership

This is the third small enterprise I have both founded and led. The personality of each enterprise has been as different as the other two, just as the leadership style that has been used and embraced is different in each case. It is hard, though, to either know or determine which environment yielded the greatest leadership successes and which environment yielded the greatest leadership failures.

There are certain constant leadership elements that cannot and should not be compromised, but the style and vigor with which they are delivered not only sets the tone and pace for the organization, but defines its unique personality as well. In other words, it would be likely for two separate organizations with the exact same leadership teams to operate with different leadership personalities. Neither would be considered less effective than the other, just different. And, since leaders are only as successful as their followers perceive them to be, leadership styles and personalities must be tailored to the teams that are being led. In the words of William Arthur Wood: "Leadership is based on inspiration, not domination; on cooperation, not intimidation."

Conveniently, we all live in the moment. And, consequently, one could argue that today's leadership styles and attributes must be most effective ones, since they are a distillation of everything that has come before them. I am not sure this is true, in large part because they are so difficult to measure, to define, and to compare.

Successful leadership must center on **impact** and **influence**. As a result, its effectiveness much depends upon the makeup of the group being led. The personalities, demeanors, characteristics, drives, tolerances, characters, idiosyncrasies, and ambitions of the group should be taken into consideration. Change is the constant, however. Leaders should manifest an embracing of a willingness to adapt, and to do so constantly. Ralph Nader stated: "I start with the premise that the function of leadership is to produce more leaders, not more followers." If the leadership goals are to impact and influence, it would be difficult to take issue with this philosophy.

Not surprisingly, I have found that merely being a "warm body at a desk" does nothing for an organization, as either a leader or as a follower. In fact, physical presence is almost irrelevant to the paradigm. Important, though, is reliable availability and ready access, which today usually manifests in the form of mobile telephone and e-mail. In other words, influence of leadership can only be successful and impactful if the leadership is "there"—not physically, necessarily, but in spirit and personality by supporting the team, providing intelligent and timely feedback, being an available sounding board, adding perspectives, and constructively nurturing, mentoring, and listening.

Leadership Resource Strategies

Over the years, I have given much thought to the concept of "resource management." Particularly, I have found it important to understand the domains over which we, as leaders, have direct or indirect control and those over which we do not. The rationale for this is that, if we can succinctly understand the influences, characteristics, relationships, interdependencies, and outcomes of each of these domains, we will likely be far more poised to influence impact and effectiveness.

As best as I have been able to determine, there are five such domains, which are time, money, people and talent, technology, and intelligence.

Time

"Half our life is spent trying to find something to do with the time we have rushed through life trying to save." – Will Rogers

Time can be both a best friend and a worst enemy. Since it is a true leader's constant, however, embracing "friendship" seems to be the only responsible and viable leadership option. There are a few simple, but very effective, requisites that not only define the efficiency of an organization being led, but that begin to manifest as a core element of the organization's culture.

As trite as it may sound, consistency of process often sets the tone for managing respective expectations. Team members being led must understand what is acceptable and what is not. An easy notion to communicate is that, since time moves on regardless, operating with purpose and conviction in an efficient manner will likely benefit all concerned, but could just as easily be squandered.

Because most businesses operate in a highly competitive, globalized environment, the efficient use of available time will likely have a marked effect on the relative success or failure of an enterprise. Some of the attributes or manifestations of an efficient use of the time resource are as follows:

To manage meetings in a time efficient manner, each meeting should be of a relatively short duration, it should have a prior communicated purpose, and it should follow a written agenda. It should begin by bringing closure to items from the associated prior meeting. With only one person speaking at a time, meeting participants should be encouraged to participate freely, without fear of subsequent retaliation: the forum should be one where all ideas and notions are fair game, regardless of popularity. They should be inspirational and informative. Part of each meeting's purpose should be for coaching, mentoring, and collaboration. Outcomes of each meeting should be documented, and individuals should be accountable to one another, the process, and the leadership.

To manage communication efficiently, responses to written and telephone communications should be as close to their receipt as is possible. Time should be set aside for a fixed period each day, so that there is a consistency and an expectation of effort. This way, time is prescheduled for project work, so it is delivered on or ahead of expectations. In addition, guessing is not an embraced protocol– if one is unsure, promise to both research and get back to the party promptly, and then do just that.

To manage standard operating procedures (SOPs) in an efficient manner, a leader should ensure that all employees are clear on how to make use of them. He or she should also review these procedures regularly and at least as often as a change is made or required. This review should ensure that standard operating procedures are not duplicative, and that they practically support the business.

Additional tips for managing time efficiently include using a written list and electronic calendar system to plan activities for the next day, week, or month that is updated daily, and using an uncomplicated and intuitive filing system for paper and electronic information. The workspace should be uncluttered, and information and documentation should be accessed quickly. It is also important to limit ad hoc and unnecessary interruptions.

Money

"Money frees you from doing things you dislike. Since I dislike doing nearly everything, money is handy." – Groucho Marx

Probably one of my biggest frustrations when dealing with others who are not financially savvy, is that there is a misconception that a profitable and growing business is self-sustaining and relatively free of demise; however, nothing could be further from the truth. For any growing and profitable business, running out of cash represents one of the greatest threats to its ongoing viability. Consequently, it is vital to be aware and to manage the business on two separate fronts: one related to profitability (revenues less costs), and one related to cash flow (money in, less money out).

For example, assume that a growing enterprise needs to upgrade its IT infrastructure, and it embarks on a series of hardware and software acquisitions that cost $360,000. Clearly, payment for these needs to take place, so there is an immediate depletion of cash to the extent of $360,000. However, from the context of profitability, it is likely that this information technology infrastructure will have a useful life of approximately thirty-six months, during which time it can be seen to have been "used up" proportionately. In this case, there will be a monthly expense charge of 1/36 of the cash cost, or $10,000. While the enterprise will likely continue to reflect a profit, it may have become completely cash depleted and at significant risk for survival.

It behooves all leaders to become educated in the finance domain, since not doing so could have dire consequences for the enterprise. The best and easiest way to do this is to develop and monitor a succinct and relevant set of performance or key indicators that should at least measure four areas.

The first area that should be measured is the relationship between revenues and balance sheet in both expanding and contracting paradigms. Secondly, the indicators should measure "fully loaded" costs. Most activities an enterprise undertakes have associated direct and indirect revenues and costs. It is important to recognize this and to be clinical about how they are determined and measured (as an example, "fully loaded" direct labor costs would likely include the following: gross compensation, including SPIFF, shift differentials, overtime, and bonus payments; employer payroll taxes; employee benefits costs paid by the employer; workers' compensation insurance; and an expense factor for paid time off). A third measurement to be taken is how hard money is being made to work by calculating return on assets, sales, and investments, and by determining what levels are minimally acceptable. Those indicators that tell a leader whether or not the enterprise is "winning" is the fourth area that should be measured and managed. Since each enterprise is different and each leadership team measures "winning" differently, these need to be individually determined.

Important, too, is to ensure that relationships with key vendors and primary bankers are proactively managed. I have found that there is more dislike and disdain for surprises than there is for bad news. A leader should communicate significant events in a timely fashion, intend for relationships to be long-term, understand available, ever-changing options, and be honest and fair.

People and Talent

"Always do right. This will gratify some people and astonish the rest." –Mark Twain

If time is the most predictable resource, people are usually the least predictable, and certainly not by design or for lack of want. However, with the "right" set of leadership tools, and the desire to empower and develop them, the impact of employees will very likely surprise you. Many of the "pearls of wisdom" I have learned appear to me to be common sense. In general, simple is better. I believe there are only a handful of concepts to be embraced, but I understand that they are the ones that have worked for me. There are very likely many others.

When hiring talent, it is important to hire the person instead of the resume. Invariably, if things do not work out, the decision driver(s) for employment termination will be related to the person, not to their skills. A leader should also hire with the expectation that the relationship will grow, that you will learn from the person, and that the encounter will be long-term.

When communicating with employees, do so constantly, effectively, and with purpose. Listen contextually, because voice tone and body language often communicate more than the words. Once a leader has listened carefully, he or she should digest and respond to the information; often, a pause or silence injects clarity. A leader should also keep communication simple by being honest, forthright, and approachable.

When managing the performance of employees, a leader should manage expectations by empowering all employees as his or her proxy within the realm of associated responsibility. Leaders should focus on the positives rather than the negatives by celebrating successes tangibly and unpredictably. Behaviors and attitudes that show integrity, as well as those that support coaching, mentoring, and collaboration, should also be rewarded. Most importantly, a leader must embrace and accept change as a constant.

Invariably, managing one or more people in an enterprise is a very fluid endeavor. However, setting the tone and the protocols for what are acceptable and unacceptable behaviors early in each relationship will go a long way to defining the culture of the enterprise. One individual will not be able to single-handedly control the entire domain; therefore, it behooves all leaders to be consistent and clear so others can act in the context of the roadmap that has been provided. If this process is performed well, there is an ever-expanding set of believers and defenders of it.

Technology

"Humanity is acquiring all the right technology for all the wrong reasons."
– R. Buckminster Fuller

One of my pet peeves is that we, as business leaders, have lost sight of technology's purpose. Traditionally, technology has been part of a complicated set of offerings that were poorly understood by those who have ultimate decision authority. It has been viewed as a "necessary evil," with expectations for high cost, relatively low impact, a long payback period, a high commitment to training, and a need to reengineer existing business processes to better enable the technology to perform.

There is also a burning desire to keep up with the "Cyber Joneses" by deploying the latest and greatest technology, coupled with the belief that it will provide a measurable competitive advantage. However, its usability is often not intuitively configured or easily integrated with other technology and systems. The technology is rarely owned, but is instead licensed for use and maintained for upgraded functionality by an outside vendor. As a result, it requires regular upgrading because of the need to stay current with operating systems, hardware, security protocols, databases, Web browsers, and software tools. These systems are also difficult to change, enhance, or customize due to the high, unpredictable costs associated with such changes.

My view is that technology should be viewed merely as a toolset that has the likely propensity to inject efficiency, consistency, and purpose into an enterprise. It requires investment and the deployment of resources such as money, people, and time. It predisposes the enterprise to better communication protocols, amalgamation of enterprise branding and marketing efforts, integrated business processes, ubiquitous access to certain data, and an ability to make more timely tactical and strategic decisions using derived information and intelligence. All that having been said, it is not the panacea, and rarely, if ever, represents a "solution." Unfortunately, this is the way it is most often positioned, reported on, and sold.

In summary, a leader's involvement in managing technology as a resource for their enterprise should return to basics. Technology, in many ways, has commoditized as it relates to price, performance, available tools, providers, differentiated vendors and technicians, hosting environments, and user perceptions. As an example, for reasons other than branding, it would be difficult to passionately defend, or to clearly differentiate, one Internet browser over another, or one accounting software application over another. In response, leaders now have an obligation to be as discerning with technology resources as they are with time, money, and people. At the very least, it should be evaluated based upon similar criteria.

Intelligence

"The world is full of willing people, some willing to work, the rest willing to let them." – Robert Frost

More so than any other resource, good leaders have the greatest influence and the most impact over the content that is produced (what), the associated processes (how), and their timing (when). We are all taught that the primary directive is for efficiency and competitive advantage. However, often the opposite manifests itself in the form of disjointed and misaligned processes, poor data from which to derive intelligent content, and bloated time budgets that have no associated accountability.

With the proliferation of the Internet, a 24/7 consumer orientation, and a large global economy, intelligence in any form is vital for the success of the enterprise. This may take the form of competitive knowledge, mined data coupled with analytics, or integrated databases. Consequently, in an effort to secure and manage the most effective business intelligence, enterprise leadership should be dedicated to embrace and support a variety of areas. Integrated technology tools that leverage intuitive and ready access to data that is usually housed in disparate repositories should receive attention. Similarly, streamlined business processes that utilize, augment, and update real-time information should be pursued.

It is important to shape a corporate culture that acknowledges and rewards the habit of gathering, disseminating, and consuming relevant information across the enterprise in as many creative legal ways as possible. Also, an environment loyal to personal growth and skills development should be encouraged by leaders. Examples of this may include exposing people to seemingly unrelated disciplines or topics, which may stimulate unexpected connections. This includes a forum, for and a willingness to, share vulnerabilities without the fear of retribution. In order to ensure this willingness, leaders should protect confidentiality and intellectual property.

It is also beneficial to regularly solicit the inputs and wisdoms of both your customers and your vendors by inviting hindsight and after-action reviews. This strategy will allow leaders to avoid making the same mistake or misstep more than once, to streamline processes, and to achieve continuous improvement.

People, for the most part, are selfishly motivated but crave to be cherished. It is the leader's job to cause the team to cherish its members so powerfully that selfish motivations are superseded with regularity and consistency of purpose.

Kevin Grauman, a founder of the Outsource Group, LLC, has served as its president and chief executive officer since its inception in 1997. He is also the founder, president, and chief executive officer of Payroll and Benefits Experts, Inc. (PBeX). PBeX was formed in 1990, and had perfected an earlier version of the business services outsourcing model that Outsource Group has adopted as its own. Kevin previously founded, and was president and chief executive officer of a regional full-service employment agency, which he sold to a national competitor in 1991. Prior to founding the aforementioned ventures, Mr. Grauman's professional experience was garnered in the public accounting arena, initially with Arthur Young & Company in Johannesburg, South Africa, and thereafter with Hood and Strong in San Francisco, California. He has a post-graduate degree in business management, and is a chartered accountant (South Africa). He was acknowledged in November of 2002 by HRO Today Magazine *as one of the "100 Superstars of HR Outsourcing in the USA," and he was recognized in Kingston's 2002 national registry of Who's Who in America. He was both a 2003 finalist for, and a 2005 winner of Ernst & Young's Entrepreneur of the Year Award.*

Mr. Grauman is regarded as a pioneer and visionary in the field of human resources outsourcing. His practical and theoretical expertise extends to financial resource management, payroll accounting, employee benefits administration, and human resources management, transliterate on local, regional, national, and international levels. He champions efficiency and compliance, primarily in favor of "non-large" employers, and regularly consults with these employers regarding wages and hours, fair employment practice, compensation, labor relations, employee benefits, and personnel management.

Dedication: *This writing is dedicated to my children, two beautiful boys, Trevor and Ryan, who are only just beginning their human journey. Like most parents for their children, I have the highest of hopes for them both. My wishes are that they become discerning of their purpose; understand and embrace fairness and equity; always recognize and acknowledge their privilege; behave and think reliably, and with honor; challenge absolutes; and conduct themselves ethically and with unrivalled integrity.*

Failure is Just Not an Option

Seth Merrin

Chief Executive Officer

Liquidnet

My Role in the Company

I see my primary role as the person who sets the direction of the company and makes sure we stay on course to ensure a successful enterprise. To accomplish this, I am continually a student of management. I am an avid reader and information junkie, and I tend to migrate toward books on leadership, management, and business improvement. I use this knowledge as a catalyst to shake up Liquidnet's management processes and responsibilities every so often. Our company's growth averages around 100 percent every year, so a top challenge is recognizing when I have to rethink my management style, and perhaps add or alter people on the management team or on my staff. Every six months, we're a different company and require a new way of looking at our business and our company's growth plans. I read just about every business magazine, newspaper, and decent business book that comes out. I find that there are always a couple of golden nuggets I can implement here. This gives me the ideas and also the energy to change and evolve.

As chief executive officer (CEO), I need to be the driver of Liquidnet's long-term vision, making sure we are constantly thinking of new revenue opportunities and how we can open ourselves to new markets. This vision must have an uncompromising focus. There are many directions a company can take, but you have to have the ability to say "no" if that direction doesn't correspond with the vision you've laid out.

I am also actively involved in our marketing area, because I believe that how we communicate our value proposition is vitally important to the company and a big part of my job. A critical aspect of leadership that is often overlooked is the need to maintain a focus on customer relationships externally, and on being the lead cheerleader internally.

Obviously, in order to be successful, a CEO must have a vision, but it takes more than that. Too many corporate visions focus on obtaining profits as their only measure of success, but they stop short of looking at how they can make a positive impact on their industry and the people they serve. Having that goal in mind makes coming to work much more rewarding and, ultimately, much more fun. As I often say to my employees, the day we stop having fun is the day we close our doors.

But it's not just about management. A good CEO must understand and commit resources to creating the best sales and marketing in his or her industry. It's been said that you can have the best product in the world, but if you have lousy people selling it, then you'll be out of business in a year. However, even if you have a mediocre product but great salespeople, then you have a shot. Luckily, Liquidnet has both a great product and sales team. We view the Liquidnet sales department as a competitive advantage in our industry. They are rigorously recruited, trained, and retrained. They must not only be experts on Liquidnet and our products, but also on the entire industry and all our competitors. Through this, they become not just pitch men and women to our customers, but colleagues and information resources they turn to.

As for marketing, too many companies separate the sales and marketing departments. This is the equivalent of having the pilot and navigator sit in two different cockpits on an airplane. At Liquidnet, marketing works alongside sales, literally sitting in the same area as the sales team. Communication between the two departments is constant, and the result is that marketing gets direct access to critical customer and prospect feedback, and can react quickly to provide the tools sales needs.

But at the core of Liquidnet's success is our product. This is also an area where I'm deeply involved. I serve on a committee called the "Roadmap Body," which meets regularly to make decisions on the future direction of our products. Our industry has money, and will try anything new, so long as it has some credibility of being successful. However, the street has very little patience—if you don't get it right the first time, you won't get a second chance.

Structured Goals Throughout the Organization

We manage in six-month periods, not five-year strategic plans. We've boiled down the areas we feel are most important overall to the business, and we focus on them as a company, departmentally, and personally, every six months. There are four components:

1. **Financial**. What do we expect our revenues to be? How many accounts do we expect to sign up? How can we cut some expenses?

2. **Corporate development**. What should we be working on in the next six months that will create a new market opportunity? What can we do today that will result in a revenue stream several years down the road?
3. **Continuous improvement**. What are the corporate and departmental areas that could use some improvement? What are some manual processes that can be automated? Where can we improve communication between departments? What are better ways of reaching our customers?
4. **Continuing education.** Every person in the organization is required to take two continuing education credits every six months; what those credits focus on is decided by that person and his or her manager.

We monitor these six-month goals very carefully. These goals are built from the bottom up. Once the departments give their goals, upper management gets together and reviews them carefully. If something is not measurable, they have to go back to the drawing board and reformulate their goals and metrics. Each department head also examines the goals of other departments and may suggest new goals of them.

Every quarter, each department goes through to find out where they are relative to those goals. These goals are wrapped up in a compensation scheme; bonuses are given twice a year, and coincide with the six-month goal process.

Working with My Team

Liquidnet's senior management meetings are run a little differently from most other companies'. Everything in the company is run and recorded in a project plan. Our management meetings focus on everybody's list of responsibilities and what they're expected to deliver within certain timeframes. We go around the table and review everything each department is supposed to get done or red flag those tasks that aren't getting done or might be late, to ensure that we are all on the same page. Since there are a lot of interdependencies, this system makes sure everyone understands what's expected of them and what they are expecting of others. It also alerts the management team to potential delays allowing for reallocation of resources early in the process.

All of Liquidnet's senior management team today has been with me since I started this company in 1999. When we look to add someone to this team, we look from within first. Obviously, they have to be highly intelligent, highly motivated, highly honest people, but so does anyone who wants to work at Liquidnet. We look for superstars that fit in with our team and our culture. It doesn't matter how smart or great you are: if you can't work within the Liquidnet culture, then you simply won't make it here. I believe you have to hire slowly, fire quickly, nurture, train, and mentor. Your key team (those who can last) are the ones you have to treat extremely well.

I tell my team to never mortgage the future for the present. Don't make any decisions that will help the short term at the expense of the longer term. I also tell people they should not get discouraged by problems that come up in business. You have to look at business as just a series of problems. How you overcome those problems is what defines you as a leader and a company.

Liquidnet insists on budget discipline. Once a year, each department develops their budget, and we expect them to plan for the unexpected. No department can go over budget. Period. If we make an exception to one, we have to make an exception to all. Overall, our discipline is to make sure we are growing revenues quarter over quarter, faster than we are growing expenses.

Generating New Ideas

During our yearly management retreat, we review all our competition and go over each one of their strengths and weaknesses. We rank our strengths and weaknesses relative to not only what our competition is doing, but to figure out what our competition could be doing: What would our strengths and weaknesses be if they did what we think would be their smartest moves? We even go to such lengths as having members of our management team take on the role of the competitor. It is then their job to try to develop a strategy that would put Liquidnet out of business. Through this, we are able to better identify Liquidnet's areas of weaknesses, and this is where we put our energy in developing new business ideas and in exploring different markets. Our bottom line philosophy with new ideas is that if we do not have the potential to be the best at it, we simply will not pursue it.

We're also very effective at segmenting our marketplace: not from a customer perspective, but from a total potential perspective. By defining how equities are traded here and in Europe, we have been able to segment where we fit in, and what the total potential is of that segment. Currently, we address 30 percent of our total potential market. Our next business initiative will help us target another 35 percent of the market, so together we have the ability to capture 65 percent of everything our customers trade. Our 2006 model is going to go after virtually all the rest.

Liquidnet has a dedicated research and development team known as our corporate strategy group. It is their job to be thinking ahead to the business opportunities we should pursue two to three years down the road. We have a list of things we want them to look at, from incremental changes to our business to pursuing whole new markets. We capture these ideas in initiative documents that are then reviewed by Liquidnet's "Roadmap Body" committee that I mentioned earlier. Many ideas are generated and discussed, but relatively few meet our disciplined criteria and move forward from concept to planning.

The main criterion for us in going after a new market is whether we can create an unfair competitive advantage. There are lots of competitors in this marketplace, but no one is doing it quite like we do. We have a value proposition that nobody compares to. As long as we can create an unfair competitive advantage, we know it would be right to enter into the marketplace. Then, we have to create an unfair, sustainable advantage. That's an extremely high bar to set, and if we haven't achieved it and our competitors can do the same thing, we know that's not the right area for us.

Top Challenges and Resources

The most challenging issue I face is maintaining the culture, values, and camaraderie of a small, entrepreneurial company while managing constant growth and change. The conventional wisdom is that the larger a company becomes, the harder it is for it to make decisions, change course, and react to unforeseen issues. I work hard to figure out ways Liquidnet can continue to be nimble and adaptable, and make sure everyone in the company understands our vision and how we all must work together to accomplish it.

An issue that is never easy is when we have to let someone go. It's possible that some people just don't fit well with Liquidnet, or that the company's needs outgrow certain people's capabilities. For the sake of employee morale and an excellent work environment, you have to be very disciplined in removing those people who are less than productive.

I don't think a lot of people understand how deep into the details I get. One misconception about me is that I'm only viewing the company from 30,000 feet. When I ask someone a detailed question, or show that I know exactly what somebody is working on, or talk in detailed terms on a product, people often are very surprised. I am a data junkie. Early on, we implemented an online analytical database, which captures everything our clients do. We track everything from sales to defect tracking and product enhancement. We then mine that data, and we can see how individual traders use our system. We then use that to help shape their behavior on our system. I look at this information as often as I can.

The Changing Role of the CEO

Today, any CEO who is not well versed in technology, how to use that technology, and what that technology can do for you, is at a serious disadvantage. One edge we have over the competition is my familiarity with technology. The role of the CEO will change as technology changes. Technology changes so quickly, and there's so much data out there, that we're moving from pull systems of data query to implementing real-time dashboards for our information systems.

I also believe the "hands off" CEO who dwells in the corner office and makes an appearance every now and then in front of the troops is a thing of the past. The CEO who inserts himself into the mix, who knows his employees on a first name basis, and who fundamentally maintains an open door policy will be the type of leader who will have the most impact. Nurture, cultivate, and reward your employees. In terms of priorities, it's your staff that is ultimately going to help you win or lose. You have to get the best staff you can get, and you have to motivate them continuously.

There are millions of decisions you have to make every day, and there's a consequence to everything you do and don't do. It's better to make a decision and be wrong then not to make a decision at all; that's the only way you're going to move the business forward. I've seen so many people who simply work on whatever the last person they spoke to wants them to work on.

Seth Merrin is founder and chief executive officer of Liquidnet Holdings, the number-one electronic marketplace for block trading. Launched on April 10, 2001, Liquidnet allows money management institutions to trade large blocks of equities directly and anonymously with significant price improvement and little to no market impact. In 2004, Liquidnet was named the fifth fastest growing private company in America according to Inc. *magazine's twenty-third annual* Inc. *500 list. Most recently,* Institutional Investor *ranked Mr. Merrin one of the top ten most influential leaders in e-finance.*

Liquidnet is the third technology firm Mr. Merrin has started. A pioneer in the trading technology industry, he led the way by delivering the industry's first order management system, the first compliance system, and the first electronic order routing system for asset managers. At first embraced only by cutting-edge firms, these technologies are now standard on virtually every trading desk in the United States.

Prior to Liquidnet, Mr. Merrin co-founded VIE Systems, Inc., a financial services application integration software company, in 1997. VIE was sold to New Era of Networks in 1999. In 1985, Mr. Merrin founded his first company, Merrin Financial, which broke new ground with its institutional trading solutions. Merrin Financial was sold to ADP in 1996. Prior to this, Mr. Merrin was a risk arbitrage trader for CIBC Oppenheimer.

Dedication: *I would like to dedicate the chapter to Anne, my wife and my soul mate and to my three superheroes, Jason, Jenna, and Jonathon.*

Developing and Following Through on a Vision

John D. Calhoun, Ph.D.

Chief Executive Officer

Integrated Management Services

The Vision

Often, employees believe chief executive officers (CEOs) really don't do "real work." However, in reality this misconception is far from the truth. There is a growing respect for leadership. While management techniques have been studied for many years, a premium is now placed on leadership—obtaining excellence from people. To me, a leader is a visionary who inspires and energizes others. This definition of leadership has two dimensions: 1. developing a vision of the future, and 2. energizing followers to make the vision reality. When a CEO has a vision, he or she must clearly delineate for followers the overall direction of the company and the collective methods of arriving at that direction. Without a vision, there is little hope for the success of a company. Vision is one of, if not the most critical trait of a leader. The leader has to have a clear idea of what he or she wants to do—professionally and personally—and the will to persevere and continue in the face of obstacles, even failure. Unless you know where you are going, it is impossible to know when you are there.

Tips for Developing a Vision

Unfortunately, a vision alone is not enough to motivate and energize people to action. Results come only if teams buy into the vision; they must believe the leader's vision is their vision—a shared vision. Only then will they accept responsibility for achieving the vision. So, the second dimension of leadership is stimulating, inspiring, or energizing the team to perform at its best.

The leader's thinking skills can be considered directional skills, because they set the direction for your organization. They provide vision, purpose, and goal definition. These are the leader's eyes and ears to the future, allowing him or her to recognize the need for change, when to make it, how to implement it, and how to manage it. Vision is found by reaching for any available reason to change, grow, and improve. Just as one performs preventive maintenance on their car, a leader must perform preventive maintenance on his or her organization. Effective leaders do not believe in the old adage, "If it ain't broke, don't fix it," because the people who do are the people who go broke. Effective leaders treat every project as a change effort. They treat every job as a new learning experience.

Effective leaders convey a very strong vision of where they want the organization to be in the future. As a leader, you have to get your people to trust you and be sold on your vision. Using the leadership tools discussed, and being honest and fair in all the leader does, will provide you with the ammunition needed to gain the team trust. To sell them on the vision, the leader needs to possess energy and display a positive attitude that is contagious.

People want a strong vision of where they are going. No one wants to be stuck in a dead-end company going nowhere, or a company headed in the wrong direction. They want to be involved with a winner. The leader must recognize that it will be his or her people who must be energized or inspired to perform at their best individually and collectively. Needless to say, it is not an easy task to get people to perform beyond what they think is possible; to routinely give an extra 25 to 35 percent. Nor is it a simple undertaking to develop a tightly knit team dedicated to excellence from a group of diverse individuals.

Leaders must create a positive attitude within their organizations. They must do this through the strength of their character and vision, and by the creation of the feeling that great things are happening in the organization. Once this feeling of optimism begins, others in the organization are moved to action. Leadership provides hope and meaning for the team; the team members begin to believe that their own future can be realized through the achievement of the organization's goals.

When setting a vision, the following points should be kept in mind:

- The vision must be realistic and attainable.
- The vision must improve the organization (morally, monetary, etc.).
- All the people should be involved in the vision-setting process.
- A program should be developed to achieve the vision.

The Six Steps of Implementing a Shared Vision

Although developing a vision can be quite a creative challenge, the process of implementing the vision can be fairly easy if the team is energized to achieve the purpose.

Step One: Vision

The first step in setting goals and priorities is to personally develop what the organization should look like at some point in the future. The mission of the organization is crucial in determining your vision. Your vision needs to coincide with the big picture. The term "vision" suggests a mental picture of what the future of the organization will look like. The concept also implies a later time horizon. This time horizon tends to be mid to long term in nature, focusing on as many as two, five, or even ten years in the future for visions affecting the entire organization. However, leaders such as supervisors or line managers tend to have shorter time horizon visions, normally six months to a year.

The concept of a vision has become a popular term within academic, government, defense, and corporate circles. This has spawned many different definitions of the term. But the vision the leader wants should be a picture of where he or she wants the organization to be at a future date. For example, try to picture what your organization would look like if it were perfect, or if the budget was reduced by 10 percent. How would you still achieve the same quality product?

Vilfredo Pareto, a nineteenth-century economist, theorized that most effects come from relatively few causes; that is, 80 percent of the effects come from 20 percent of the possible causes. For example, 20 percent of the inventory items in the supply chain of an organization accounts for 80 percent of the inventory value.

Some leaders fall into the time-wasting trap of going after the 80 percent of items that only have a value of 20 percent of the total net worth. The leader's vision needs to picture the 20 percent that will have the greatest impact on their organization. Although it is nice to have small victories every now and then by going that easy 80 percent, spend the majority of your time focusing on the few things that will have the greatest impact—that is what a good leader does.

Once the leader has vision, it needs to be framed in general, measurable terms and communicated to the team. The team then develops the ends (objectives), ways (concepts), and means (resources) to achieve the vision.

Step Two: Goals

The second step involves establishing goals, with the active participation of the team. Goals are also stated in measurable terms, but they are more focused. For example, "The organization must reduce transportation costs." This establishes the framework of the leader's vision.

Step Three: Objectives

Definable objectives provide a way of measuring the movement towards vision achievement. This is the real strategy of turning visions into reality. It is the crossover mechanism between the leader's forecast of the future and the envisioned, desired future. Objectives are stated in precise, measurable terms such as, "By the end of the next quarter, the shipping department will use one parcel service for shipping items under a hundred pounds, and one motor carrier for shipping items over a hundred pounds." The aim is to get general ownership by the entire team.

Step Four: Tasks

The fourth step is to determine tasks. Tasks are the means for accomplishing objectives. Tasks are concrete, measurable events that must occur. An example might be, "The transportation coordinator will obtain detailed shipping rates from at least ten motor carriers."

Step Five: Timelines

This step establishes a priority for the tasks. Since time is precious and many tasks must be accomplished before another can begin, establishing priorities helps your team determine the order in which the tasks must be accomplished, and by what date. For example, "The shipping rates will be obtained by May 9."

Step Six: Follow-Up

The final step is to follow up, measure, and check to see if the team is doing what is required. This kind of leader involvement validates that the stated priorities are worthy of action. For the leader, it demonstrates his or her commitment to see the matter through to a successful conclusion. Also, note that validating does not mean to micro-manage. Micro-management places no trust in others, whereas following up determines if the things that need to get done are in fact getting done.

Then, a CEO must enforce this vision on both an internal and external level. The inside tasks include motivating and inspiring others to believe in his or her vision.

Leaders are very important for three basic reasons. First, leaders are responsible for the effectiveness of organizations. The success or failure of organizations, whether it is the church, the school, the manufacturing plant, or the movie theater, rests on the quality of leadership. The stock prices rise and fall according to the public perception of how good the leader is.

The second reason is that the change and upheaval of the past few years has left us with need for cover. People need anchors in their lives, and leaders fill that need.

Third, with the fall of national and international powerhouses such as Enron, WorldCom, and Tyco, there is a pervasive national concern about the integrity of our institutions. Wall Street was, not long along, where a man's word was his bond. The recent events and indictments have forced the industry to change the way it conducted business for more than 150 years. Mergers and acquisitions, deregulation, information technologies, and global competition are altering how business is being conducted. Changing demographics, escalating consumer sophistication, and new needs are altering the marketplace. Changing industry structures, new strategic alliance, new technologies and modes, and stock market volatility are altering the ways we conduct business.

Many leaders are at a loss on how to make their employees more productive, longing for the sort of power that would force them to produce more.

The economic climate has forced leaders to tighten the organizational belt. Organizations are downsizing. Remaining staff is forced to do more with less. The employees feel the uncertainty and strain as they work harder and longer, and worry whether their own jobs will be the next to go.

The fact is, the leader can take control. The way the leader handles himself or herself can mean the difference between an atmosphere of fear and blame, and one of confidence and cooperation.

Some suggestions for the leader:

- Set an example. Attitude from above can be crucial when the emotional climate at the top is negative; it sets the tone for subordinates. The leader can set the example for employees of tolerance, understanding, and support.
- Speak clearly, listen closely. When an organization is under stress, rumors abound and tempers run slant, so the leader must have clear communication in order to clear up rumors before they grown and become unmanageable.
- Avoid apologies. The leader undoubtedly will have to ask more of his or her staff than normally found equitable. In this event, an apologetic stance can be just as unproductive as one that shows resentment. Both attitudes are de-motivators, and they diminish the respect the leader needs in order to lead effectively.
- Purchasing power. The amount of goods, services, and real property obtainable by working in this country ranks close to the top on a world scale.
- More money, not only in the form of raises, but also from profit sharing and stock-purchasing plans, is still a powerful incentive that can be used to boost productivity.
- Recognition and reward. The employee who does superior work will continue to do so if he or she senses that the company recognizes and appreciates the effort. The leader can foster productive behavior by judiciously meting out praise, increased responsibility, and promotions. Encouragement and upward mobility rank high in the hierarchy of incentives.
- Participative management. Employee self-interest and organizational goals tend to merge when employees can participate in decision-making and decision-implementing processes.

- Create a supportive environment. In the book *In Search of Excellence*, Thomas Peters and Robert Waterman, Jr. cite a study that randomly asked adults to rank themselves on "the ability to get along with others." According to Peters and Waterman, all the participants ranked themselves in the top 10 percent, and "26 percent thought they were in the top 1 percent of the population." In the same study, 70 percent rated themselves in the top 25 percent in terms of leadership.

Peters and Waterman stated that excellent companies make their people feel like winners. They said, "Their people, by and large, make their targets and quotas because [these] are set—often by the people themselves—to allow that to happen." Peters and Waterman point to a major company "which explicitly manages to ensure that 70 to 80 percent of its salespeople meet quotas, in contrast to a less successful competitor at which only 40 percent of its sales force meets its quotas in a given year." With this approach, at least 60 percent of the salespeople think of themselves as losers. Label someone a loser, and they'll start acting like one.

There are several lessons that can be learned from this. People tend to act in accordance with their self-image. If they see themselves as well regarded, they will work to perpetuate this image. The leader must be supportive. Praise, appreciation, respect, new responsibilities, delegated authority, bonuses, raises—all are rewards from the leaders that can't help but play a crucial role in boosting employees' self-esteem and productivity.

Inspiring Your Employees

Getting people to accomplish something is much easier if they have the inspiration to do so. Inspire means "to breathe life into." And in order to perform that, we have to have some life ourselves. Three main actions will aid you in accomplishing this:

1. Be passionate. In organizations where there is a leader with great enthusiasm about a project, a trickle down effect will occur. You must be committed to the work you are doing. If you do not communicate excitement, how can you expect your people to get worked up about it?

2. Get your employees involved in the decision-making process. People who are involved in the decision-making process participate much more enthusiastically than those who just carry out their boss's order. Help them contribute, and tell them you value their opinions. Listen to them, and incorporate their ideas when it makes sense to.

3. Know what your organization is about. The fundamental truth, as General Creighton W. Abrams used to say in the mid-1970s, is that "the Army is not made up of people. The Army is people. Every decision we make is a people issue." Your organization is the same; it may make a product or sell a service, but it is still people. A leader's primary responsibility is to develop people and enable them to reach their full potential. Your people may come from diverse backgrounds, but they all have goals they want to accomplish. Create a "people environment" where they truly can be all they can be.

Outside of the organization, a CEO must repeat the vision to customers in an effort to convince them that the particular company provides the very best services possible.

Being a Successful Leader

There is a difference between leaders and managers. Every organization needs both. Leaders are needed to light the way of the future and inspire people to achieve excellence. Managers are essential to ensure that day-to-day operations run smoothly, and that the assets of the organization, both human and physical, are cared for and protected. Managers tend to stress organization, coordination, and control of resource. Managers focus on the achievement of short-term objectives and goals.

In contrast, leaders tend to stress relationships with others, values, commitment, and the spiritual component of the organization. A successful CEO with good leadership skills also has good listening skills and good interpersonal skills. He or she must be able to see the unseen and believe in the impossible. All leaders need to have the capacity to create a compelling vision, one that takes people to a new place, and to translate that vision into reality. Seeing the unseen and believing in the impossible that is not understood remains a mere occurrence. Max DePree, in *Leadership is an Art*, wrote, "The first responsibility of a leader is to define reality. The last is to say thank you. In between, the leader is a servant."

The leader also articulates a vision of the goals an organization can achieve in the short and long term. Leaders move the organization in new directions because they are unsatisfied with maintaining the status quo. They empower people to act on their own to achieve objectives and to set standards higher than previous ones. They favor taking risks, making changes, recreating or setting new paradigms, and generating a feeling of meaning in work. Last but not least, leaders need an insatiable passion to develop themselves continuously. This passion must be backed with conviction and belief. Higher-performing leaders exhibit exceptional determination in pursuing their objectives. They never give up until they succeed. Passion is a basic ingredient of leadership. The leader loves what he or she does, and loves doing it. The leader can energize employees by communicating passion. Passion gives hope and inspiration to others. Often, when the odds are against you, passion helps.

Working with Other Executives

I work very closely with the president, or chief operating officer, of the company. These positions often overlap, because the president deals with the day-to-day operations while I deal with long-term strategies and the overall picture. We overlap because there is no picture if a CEO does not understand what is happening today. Understanding what is going on in the organization is really important for me. He also has to deal with clients and with getting people to understand where the organization is going, both internally and externally. It is important that both of us work with the same intensity and a true commitment to making a difference in the lives of the employees, and in the lives of the communities we serve. We both try to promote communication among employees as well as between the company and the communities we serve.

Necessary Skills of a Team Member

The most important resource for a company is its people. I believe in the power of people, in the power of networking, and in the value of making friendships. Some would argue that all leaders must have charisma, and either you have it or you don't. But I have met leaders who would not be described as being very charismatic, yet these leaders were able to inspire and motivate. And through their abilities to motivate, and get people on their side, they were able to effect needed change in their organizations. In order to do that, the people following must honestly believe in the person they are following and that following is the right thing to do at the time. The informal network in a company is just as important as the formal network. Much of the leader's success depends on the willingness of employees to help by providing information and support for the program. During times of crisis, this support becomes increasingly important. Needless to say, if you make a serious mistake or results falter, you need others to rally behind you.

As a result, the skills of a team member are important to a company. At IMS, team members must be willing to take the initiative by making things happen and by not being afraid of risk. Team members must also understand that the leadership at IMS talks about creating possibilities and doing what is impossible. Individuals that are members of this team must have a "can do" term attitude that involves facing obstacles and overcoming them.

Setting and Monitoring Team Goals

Every year, the company has a goal-setting seminar workshop assignment in which key management sits down with the team to discuss the goals and targets the company should achieve in the upcoming year. Our employees are encouraged to participate. We've developed a mastermind group that consists of employees on every level. In order to monitor these goals, the company uses measurements and time tables for achieving those objectives.

Successful Strategies

In order to achieve success, the strategy of any company should be to develop relationships with its customers. In most industries, numerous companies offer competitive services or products that provide clients with a variety of choices. As a result, potential customers must feel confident and comfortable in the ability of a company. They also want you to care about them, and this is the leadership we're bringing to the table.

Another successful strategy is setting the tone of the company by being an example for others to follow. This involves maintaining a cheerful attitude and working environment. Employees cannot work under stress; as a result, the CEO should try to have fun so others will do the same. This strategy also involves recognizing that a single person cannot know everything, and that mistakes are inevitable. By creating this environment, employees can see the human side of their leaders.

Leaders must be willing to say "I made a mistake" or "I don't know." If the leader criticizes an employee and later discovers that he or she was actually correct, the leader should immediately go to that person and apologize for the error. Leaders who are unable to own mistakes place their own welfare above that of the organization.

Overcoming Challenges

One of a CEO's biggest challenges is fostering belief in a particular vision. Many employees have been bamboozled in organizations to the extent that they have almost given up hope. As a leader, a CEO must make others believe conditions will improve. Regardless of the organization, the tough economic times are causing companies to operate on less and less. In the past, one person has been doing the jobs of two people; now, he or she is doing the jobs of three people. To maintain the belief that they are winners day after day in these conditions is a challenge. However, effective leaders combat this challenge by building cohesiveness and pride in the organization. One of the secrets of effective leadership is to promote employee communications and motivational programs with the same intensity as marketing to customers. One of the best ways to create employee awareness of a heroic goal is through symbols and slogans. To be effective, they must be unusual and catchy.

An effective leader is tough-minded when it comes to obtaining results from subordinates. Excuses are not tolerated when achievable goals are not met. What counts are results, and that the person really tried. If an employee does not measure up after retraining and repeated warnings, the leader must have the fortitude to take appropriate disciplinary action.

Expenses

The largest expenses for IMS are personnel costs, new hires, benefits, and health insurance. Additional money is spent based upon the priorities and goals the company set for the year. The goals and the financing for those goals are directly aligned.

Recently, IMS purchased new corporate offices and spent a large amount of money renovating these offices. The amount spent was included in the capital improvements budgets.

Research and Development

As a leader, it is important to demand new ways to break away from the status quo. Leaders should constantly challenge employees by asking them to invent new processes, new ideas, new concepts, and new inventions that will improve the company. In the engineering industry, firms are constantly working to benchmark the progress of the company, as well as to create innovative ideas. They also strive to create an organization in which learning through innovation occurs on a daily basis.

A CEO's Changing Role

Because I have been in the role of CEO for nine years, I have not seen the role change drastically, other than the technology matters that have been introduced to the marketplace. The only change has been the increased speed at which business operates due to this technology. The same decision-making skill set that was used when Alexander Graham Bell invented the telephone is still in place. The people may have changed, but they still want to be treated with respect, happiness, and honesty. They still want information openly and willingly shared with them.

In the future, however, technology will decrease the number of people in the workplace. I see a widening of the haves and have-nots. There also has to be more of a sense of urgency in the future. A leader does things others dare not do. He or she does things in advance of other people, and makes new things or makes old things look new. Having learned from the past, he or she lives in the present, with eyes on the future. And strangely, each leader puts it together in a totally different way. The effective leader has a strong sense of urgency. The attitude has to be, "Let's do it, and let's do it now!"

In order to achieve success in any context, a CEO must first be committed to doing the best job possible. Secondly, he or she should build a staff with the highest quality people. A third point is being willing to admit mistakes and uncertainty.

John D. Calhoun, Ph.D. is chief executive officer of Integrated Management Services (IMS). IMS divisions include IMS Engineers (the third-largest 100 percent African-American-owned engineering firm in the nation), IMS Technical Institute, and IMS Autrans (a tier one supplier for Nissan North America). IMS was recently named to the prestigious Inc. *500 list as one of America's fastest growing companies. IMS came in at number 183 with a five-year sales growth of 908 percent. IMS' client list includes the likes of Nissan North America, the United States Department of Defense, the United States Department of Agriculture, the United States Army Corps of Engineers, Jackson International Airport, Hinds County, the Motorola Corporation, the Mississippi Department of Transportation, the Mississippi State Bureau of Building, Grounds and Real Property Management, Wal-Mart Corporation, the City of Jackson, the City of New Orleans, the City of Memphis, and the City of Detroit.*

Dr. Calhoun is a product of Jackson Public School, and is a graduate of Memphis State University, where he received his bachelor's and master's degrees. He also received his master's degree in business administration from Jackson State University, and his Ph.D. from the University of Mississippi. Dr. Calhoun did post-doctoral executive education studies at the Tuck School of Business at Dartmouth, the Center for Closely Held Firms of the Sellinger School of Loyola University, and the University of Texas at El Paso.
Dr. Calhoun has authored or co-authored several published articles including: "The Impact of Financial Appropriations on Desegregation Activities and Enhancement Efforts at Mississippi's Historically Black Public University" in the Academy of Management Journal, *"Organizational Culture in Local Governments" in the* Journal of Business Administration, *and "Contaminated Groundwater Impact on Economic and Community Development" in the Proceedings of the National Forum for Black Public Administrator.*

Prior to founding IMS, Dr. Calhoun served as the senior advisor for the mayor of the city of Jackson, Mississippi, where he was the chief architect for the creation of the Metro Jackson Housing Partnership and the Jackson Hinds MINCAP fund, an institution that lends millions of dollars to minority businesses. Dr. Calhoun also served on the management faculty in the School of Business at Jackson State University. He was one of the founding board members of Big Brother/Big Sisters of the Tri-County Area, and serves on the YMCA board of directors. He is a member of the American Management Association, the National Forum for Black Public Administrators, the International City Managers Association, the Academy of Business Administrators, and the Leadership Jackson Alumni Association.

Dr. Calhoun is committed to revitalizing the inner city. He is a member of Alpha Phi Alpha Fraternity, and has received numerous awards for his community involvement, including YMCA Citizen of the Year, the Jackson Public Schools VAST Award, the Volunteer Award from Boys and Girls Club of America, and many others.

Dr. Calhoun attends Miracle Temple Church, where he serves as the church administrator and trustee. He is the son of the Reverend and Mrs. T.J. Calhoun, and is the very proud father of Tracy Alexander-Calhoun, affectionately known as Paco, who attends St. Mary's Catholic School.

Dedication: *To my business partner, Rod, who puts up with my craziness, and to Paco, who I love dearly.*

The Goals and Responsibilities of Every CEO

Jay Steinmetz

Chief Executive Officer

Barcoding Inc.

My Ultimate Goal

The goal of a chief executive officer (CEO) is to be the visionary who determines the direction that will achieve the best long-term return on investment for the market base of a company. As a result, the CEO affects the company financially in a variety of aspects. By determining the execution strategies on a macro scale, a CEO allows a company to generate the revenue that will maintain its existence. A CEO must direct the company so as to maximize long-term value by forecasting the future market trends. Frequently, CEOs participate in business development, strategic technology, and goal strategies, as well as makes presentation appearances. For example, a CEO could direct a company toward radio frequency identification or spectrum analysis in the wireless propagation testing, depending on which investment would be more profitable.

The Art of Being a CEO

A difference exists between a CEO and a successful CEO. On a micro scale, almost any individual can run a business and be somewhat successful. In order to achieve a macro execution strategy, however, an individual needs to think in ways that allow others to maximize their potential. In order for a CEO to be successful, he or she must be motivated, positive, detail-oriented, driven, personable, and charismatic. Talent is important, but without business savvy, a CEO could not survive.

Different levels of CEOs exist, from extremely successful ones in a small business to those with successful visions on a large scale. There are many CEOs that can sell well and execute well on a micro level. If a CEO wants his or her company to become a multimillion-dollar one, however, he or she must build an organization that can run itself. The only purpose of a successful CEO of a large corporation should be on a longer-term strategic guidance level.

The best advice for a CEO is learning to become process-based. Every position needs to be documented and measured with specific criteria that get evaluated weekly, monthly, quarterly, and yearly. A significant amount of points are rewarded just for reporting, and the rest is performance-based.

My director of marketing gets points for customer press releases, points for monthly newsletters, and so on.

CEOs should also involve themselves in political and organizational structures. This involvement allows them to leverage the relationships or information discovered to produce more sales for the company.

Successful Strategies and Methodologies

A successful strategy for a CEO is to remain positive, especially in front of the outside world. Additionally, CEOs must show excitement and interest in a company in order to promote these qualities in the people that surround them.

Another successful strategy to pursue is focusing on the core strengths of a business and being aggressive in achieving those strengths. A CEO must understand the business and the marketplace in order to create a process for which he or she then executes. This process must manage people and provide them with the tools and the grading system to show them that they are achieving the goals set for them.

Maintaining business partnerships is a successful strategy, because it enables companies to partner with others that have complimentary technology. For example, Barcoding, Inc., is partnering with Oracle on a project in which Barcoding does the hardware while Oracle does the software.

Another strategy is geographic expansion. By utilizing franchises, a company can expand geographically while simultaneously giving individuals partial control of their own domain. In this business relationship, the parent company processes all the orders while the franchise owner hires individuals and takes advantage of the profits remaining after franchising fees.

Overcoming Challenges

A CEO must negotiate the line between obtaining the tentative approval of a company and being in control of the company. In some cases, CEOs must make the tough decision to execute a strategy that is not liked by all involved parties. Particularly, the decision to fire employees is difficult; however, a CEO would not survive without the confidence to do what is best for a company, regardless of the difficulty of the decision. In order to overcome these challenges, CEOs must understand how different people will react to a decision. If it will break them, a CEO will have to badger them continually about a subject to the point that they finally relent. Frequently, it is useful with some individuals to give them the appearance that they are making the decisions while subtly shifting them in the appropriate direction.

The most difficult challenge for a CEO is retaining good people. In order to overcome this challenge, employees must be challenged, but also must have enough autonomy, compensation, and team collaboration to ensure that they will remain with a company. Fostering a sense of community also helps by hosting social and sporting events outside the office.

Misconceptions also pose challenges: the biggest misconception about the CEO is that he or she actually runs the company. Instead, the role of a CEO is to create an organization that runs itself. The people underneath CEOs are beholden to them to visualize strategies; however, they can run the organization in many ways if they can achieve those directives. When a CEO is working effectively, he or she can disappear for a week without a cell phone and/or laptop with little or no consequences.

Working with Other Executives

CEOs work closely with the controller, the executive vice president, and the director of marketing of a company. A CEO must have trust in his or her management to understand the complexities of the employees they are managing. How the manager chooses to interact with employees may be different in style than the CEO, as long as positive metrics are obtained from the careful documentation of process controls that are put in place. If the management has the proper direction, documentation, and execution strategy, then communications with the CEO will just be for positive feedback.

Team Members

A team member must posses the ability to make decisions and read individuals. He or she must understand and interpret what other people are thinking in order to make decisions. The chief operating officer (COO) must make sure all the gears are working well.

A meeting is held to discuss what needs to be accomplished by the company, how to accomplish it, and the goals required of a particular department. At the beginning of a quarter, individuals are then assigned particular goals. In marketing, a goal may be as simple as a successful tradeshow. With operations, it may be the integration of order entry and customer relationship management.

In order to ensure that goals are being met, a company should organize weekly meetings in which the CEO goes through a list of tasks to see if people are accomplishing them. Goals that are not met are directly associated with points that equivocate to a reduced bonus.

Research and Development

For research and development, a company can have students who do preliminary research, and then it can conduct meetings to determine how much further it needs to go. After obtaining the research, a company analyzes the market through a market analysis and an industrial analysis. Then a particular product or project is voted upon to see if the senior executives want to pursue the project by ranking it compared to current ones.

Reading external publications and gauging customer trends in purchasing are two additional important resources to determine direction.

Changing Role of the CEO

CEOs will continue to operate on the strategic, structural level. The only difference is that technology is changing faster and, as a result, a CEO needs to be more reactionary. In order to continue successfully in the future, a CEO must remember three general rules: you can't always speak your mind; you have to know all the details before reacting; and it is not that it happened, but why it happened that is important.

Barcoding Inc., a full-service technology company, sells automated data collection solutions, utilizing wireless and handheld technology, to business customers.

Jay Steinmetz's entrepreneurial career began at the University of Arizona in the prestigious Berger Entrepreneurship Program. Designed to teach all aspects of starting a business, from the original idea to opening the doors for the first time, the program highlighted the entrepreneurial skills of Mr. Steinmetz by inducting him into its Hall of Fame in the summer of 2002.

With a degree in inventory management, Mr. Steinmetz was hired by the Department of Defense to write computer programs for tracking highly valuable and sensitive equipment. Looking for the most efficient and accurate system, Mr. Steinmetz developed a system utilizing barcoding technology. The managers of the data collection company contracted to supply the barcode equipment were so impressed with his ability to develop that they hired him to design barcoding application systems for their customers. While employed, Mr. Steinmetz tried to convince the company to invest more in the Internet, but when he was unsuccessful, his entrepreneurial spirit led him to do it on his own. In 1997, he founded the company known today as Barcoding.

The Baltimore Business Journal *honored Mr. Steinmetz in 2001 as a "Top 40 Business Leader Under 40." In 2004, Barcoding became an* Inc. *500 company and was recognized by* Forbes *magazine as one of ten privately held technology companies to watch. Known for his entrepreneurial skills, he has been called upon to write guest columns in nationally published industry magazines, and is frequently used as a media source for information on wireless, mobile, and handheld technology.*

C-LEVEL BUSINESS INTELLIGENCE
ASPATORE
BOOKS
C-LEVEL BUSINESS INTELLIGENCE